DISCOVER YOUR |

ENTRUSTED

ANCHORING YOUR LIFE IN THE GOSPEL

DAVID SHIBLEY

Cover art by Jonathan Bailey/Lightstock
www.lightstock.com/

Burkhart Books
www.burkhartbooks.com
Bedford, Texas

"I'm grateful for this treasure of a resource developed by my father. *Entrusted* is a wonderful reminder and exhortation for all of us to prize, protect, and pursue the greatest gift of all—the gift of the gospel.

– **Jonathan Shibley**, President
Global Advance

"Both the spiritual stability and virility of David Shibley's creative and globally impacting ministry provide the depth of perspective and sensitivity that undergirds the maturity he has and demands. *Entrusted* addresses the erosion of substance and shallowness of grasp of the gospel among far too many today. I know of no ministry that exceeds the wisdom and strategy of fruitfulness in providing transformational teaching and equipping of leaders. I commend David and Global Advance to all who would support the testimony of Jesus and the clear message of God's holy word until the Savior comes."

– **Jack W. Hayford**, Chancellor
The King's University

"I have respected the work of David Shibley for years and have looked to him as a key leader in the global mission of the Christian faith. In his latest book, *Entrusted*, he gives great clarity to the gospel and its power to transform the culture. His faithfulness to the cause of Christ deserves our attention and respect."

– **Rice Broocks**, Author of *God's Not Dead*
Every Nation Ministries

"David Shibley is considered by many to be one of the leading missionary statesmen of our time. His new book, *Entrusted*, brings critically needed clarity to the source and impact of gospel of Christ.

– **Jim Burkett**, Director
Apologetics on Fire

"*Entrusted* is a clarion call to this generation to recapture the essence and power of the gospel. David Shibley brings a lifetime of faithful commitment to the proclamation of the good news to bear upon this vital issue. The careful, prayerful reading of this text will impact the direction of your life and ministry.

– **Scott Camp**, Evangelist, Educator
Scott Camp Ministries

"David Shibley has reminded every believer that we have been *entrusted* with the greatest news ever. We have no right to change or rearrange it, only the right to proclaim it—and proclaim it we must!"

– **E. Howard Conatser**, President
Church on the Rock Network of Ministers

"History's greatest apostle once declared, "I am not ashamed of the gospel...." Now a leader of today's global church, Dr. David Shibley, *entrusted* with that same gospel, has proclaimed it, explained it, and demonstrated its power not only in this book but in over 60 nations of the world. Read on! Be changed!

– **Amos Dodge**, Senior Pastor
Capital Church

"The message of the gospel is the 'Mount Everest' of human history and the focal point of all eternity. I am so thankful to David Shibley for a life of fidelity to the gospel. This book is merely an expression of his lifetime passion for Christ, his acute theological precision, and his unswerving devotion to the noble task of world evangelization. I urge every Christian: imbibe deeply of its transforming message."

– **Mike Downey**, President
Strategic Impact

"In a time when the meaning of the gospel has often become muddled and incoherent, David Shibley issues a clarion and compelling call to look freshly and faithfully at the good news of God's great salvation in Jesus. This is a book for those who have a deep passion for biblical fidelity, as well as intellectual and spiritual honesty concerning what it truly means to repent, believe, and be transformed by the gospel. The material presented here is deeply rich and will be dynamically rewarding to the careful reader. May God bless this book and send its timely and timeless message to everyone, everywhere."

– **Dale Evrist**, Senior Pastor
New Song Christian Fellowship

"What I love the most about David Shibley is that he has always kept the main thing the main thing. While so much of the church chases distracting sideshows, David always calls us to the core of the gospel—and the imperative of evangelism. It would be a good idea for all of us to read this book once a year, just to make sure we haven't veered off course. This book will help you focus your life on God's primary passion."

– **J. Lee Grady,** former editor of *Charisma*
The Mordecai Project

"G. K. Chesterton once said, 'People reject the idea of original sin when it is the only doctrine of Christianity that can be empirically proven.' And, indeed, the daily headlines confirm the grim truth that something is desperately wrong with humanity, and with our world. In this bracing volume my friend David Shibley persuasively diagnoses the problem and winsomely describes the solution—the good news of Jesus Christ, applied to all of life. For a fresh dose of encouragement on how to share this good news, don't miss *Entrusted!*

– **Stan Guthrie**, Editor at Large
The Chuck Colson Center for Christian Worldview

"When Dr. David Shibley writes a book, I order a copy right away. His passion for the lost and his heart for missions inspire me to do big things for

God. As a senior missionary statesman, he has impacted nations around the world with his strategic thinking and innovative approach to discipleship. In this book he explains the true meaning of the gospel of Jesus Christ. Read it! You will discover simple yet profound truths that will challenge your thinking and change your life."

– **Daniel King,** President
King Ministries International

"I am so proud to know and serve with David Shibley. He has lived his life with Scripture as his guide. He has dedicated himself to the work of the kingdom, responding to the call of Jesus to 'go and make disciples of all the nations.' David has lived this action call of the gospel, and this book will inspire you to respond to that same call!"

– **Todd Lane**, Executive Senior Pastor
Gateway Church

"*Entrusted* will help you clarify priorities and live passionately for what matters most in life!"

– **Dale O'Shields**, Senior Pastor
Church of the Redeemer

"In *Entrusted*, David Shibley shows you how to make the gospel central to your life. Reading this book will transform the Great Commission into your commission to take the gospel to your street, your neighborhood, and your city. God trusts us so much that He has *entrusted* us with this glorious gospel. *Entrusted* will enable you to know that God believes in you."

– **Gordon Robertson**, CEO
The Christian Broadcasting Network

"At a critical time David Shibley has written a masterpiece. We have been *entrusted* with a simple yet profound message that must be proclaimed with accuracy. The eternity of the masses and the effectiveness of the church depend on this. Dr. Shibley has shared with us not only his expansive knowledge but his passion for those whose lives hang in the balance."

– **Eldred Sawyer**, Executive Director
Care Center Ministries

"As I look at my bookshelf, I have many books I know I will throw away one day. Yet, I have certain books that will be handed down to my children and grandchildren. They have stood the test of time and are as powerful today as in the day they were written. My lifelong friend, David Shibley, has written a new book, *Entrusted: Anchoring Your Life in the Gospel*. It is another in a long line of books he has written giving biblical wisdom that will endure for years to come. Read and be blessed."

– **Bob Yandian**, President
Bob Yandian Ministries

ACKNOWLEDGMENTS

Many people have helped turn the vision for this, my most important book, into reality.

I want to start by acknowledging my parents, Warren and Lillian Shibley. They are both home with the Lord. They created a gospel culture for me and my sisters that wrapped us in joy, grace, assurance, and purpose. To have my formative years enveloped in the gospel and its attendant blessings is a gift beyond price.

I'm grateful to work with a wonderful team at Global Advance. All of them have been great encouragers for this project. One of the greatest joys of my life is to serve with our son, Jonathan, to advance the cause of Christ in our time. Kathy Stevens helped move this project along in ways large and small. Global Advance's international network of church leaders also gave much appreciated encouragement, spurring me by their statements of the need for this book worldwide. I'm profoundly grateful for the partners of Global Advance who have undergirded the vision with their prayers and support. My heartfelt thanks to all our team for their affirmation.

Special mention must go to Roger and Charlotte Merschbrock, prayer coordinators for Global Advance, and our ministry's prayer team. Several people have joined them in concerted prayer regarding this book. Our prayer team stayed vigilant throughout every stage of this book's development. During times when the project seemed dormant they pursued in prayer and words of encouragement to me. Their faith is now made sight.

Meeting Tim Taylor as I was in the early stages of the book's development was sovereignly ordained. Tim's father, Jack Taylor, was one of the foremost leaders of the renewal movement among Southern Baptists. He remains a highly respected church leader today. Tim's work as publisher has been invaluable. I'm very grateful to partner with Burkhart Books on this project. The content of this book is wrapped in a beautiful, compelling cover designed by Jonathan Bailey, co-founder of Lightstock.

Many friends in ministry encouraged me along the way. I'm particularly grateful for the encouragement I've received from Dale Evrist and Brad Howard. I owe a debt of thanks to each colleague in ministry who provided an endorsement. My special thanks to Jim Burkett, Scott Camp, Ken Foley, Ron Minth, and Hallie Powers for helping edit and proof these pages. I also want to express my thanks to the launch team that will help give this book the audience its contents deserves.

Through the years I've written articles and books published by Charisma Media. I express my thanks to Steve Strang for permission to draw from my thoughts and writings that have been published over the years through several channels of Charisma Media.

The deepest thanks is reserved for my greatest partner in life and ministry. Naomi and I have walked together with Jesus for over four decades. She is the consummate minister's wife. Naomi has been abundantly supportive. Many nights I've written well past midnight. She never complained, always staying cheerful and encouraging. I love her with all my heart. She has brought me favor from the Lord.

Intense spiritual battle has surrounded this book's completion. The Lord has sustained me. No doubt more battles, and more victories, are ahead. May multitudes walk with Jesus and live with Him forever because of this book's impact. May God the Father, Son, and Holy Spirit be adored and the gospel be adorned through the ministry of this book.

CONTENTS

But as we have been approved by God to be entrusted with the gospel, even so we speak, not as pleasing men, but God who tests our hearts.

1 Thess. 2:4

. . . the glorious gospel of the blessed God which was committed to my trust.

1 Tim.1:11

For if I preach the gospel, that gives me no ground for boasting. For necessity is laid upon me. Woe to me if I do not preach the gospel! For if I do this of my own will, I have a reward, but if not of my own will, I am still entrusted with a stewardship.

1 Cor. 9:16-17, ESV

INTRODUCTION

The warm Oklahoma sun drenched my car as I set out on a personal pilgrimage. I wanted—I needed—to connect with my spiritual heritage.

I had been busy, very busy. Busy in worthy endeavors, frenetically doing God's work. Yet I was feeling adrift. Unwittingly, I had somehow detached my efforts from their source and purpose. There was plenty of activity but little focus. I needed to recover roots and reasons for all the exertion. I needed to retrieve non-moving moorings and drop a surely-embedded anchor.

Arriving in the small town of Drumright I parked the car and ascended the steps to the old auditorium of the First Baptist Church. Sitting on the top step I could almost feel heaven's mercy drops sprinkling my parched spiritual terrain. I wept and worshiped. Almost a century earlier the young man who would become my grandfather and the young woman who would be my grandmother were married here. And it was here they heard the gospel.

Both came from immigrant families and austere religious backgrounds. But at the Baptist church in Drumright they heard and embraced the good news of God's salvation through faith in Jesus Christ. Through that church's ministry they discovered a real relationship with a living Redeemer. Not only did these young, new Americans have a new home, they had a new birth, a new life. And for our family everything began to change.

Continuing my odyssey I drove some twenty miles to Bristow. I went to the property the Assembly of God congregation occupied in the 1930s. The sprinkle became a shower as the gospel's glory rained down on my heart again. It was at this church that the young man who later became my dad heard the good news of God's redeeming love and committed his life to Christ. Once again everything changed—for Warren Shibley and for his future family.

The final leg of my journey took me to Tulsa and the church where I first opened my heart to Jesus in Vacation Bible School. I walked inside and drank in the memories. God's refreshing shower became a torrent of gratitude gushing through me. The auditorium looked much the same as it did then. I sat in the empty auditorium and memories transported me back to that Day of days. I recalled Mrs. Gertrude Nathan, looking like the quintessential Vacation Bible School teacher in her cotton dress and wire rim glasses, telling The Big Story. My mind jumped to the next scene where somehow I had left my seat and joined other children kneeling at an old-time altar at the front of the church. Mrs. Nathan was leading us into that life-altering heart surrender:

Lord Jesus,

Thank You for dying on the cross for me. Right now, I turn away from all my sins and I receive You as my Savior. Come into my heart, Lord Jesus. Take my sins away, Dear God, I want to be Your child from now on. Jesus, I want to follow You as my Lord. Let me love You and live for You all the days of my life.

Amen.

Now these decades later I had returned to this sacred site, the place where I first came to God through simple faith in His Son. I knelt at the spot where I trusted Christ as my Savior and bowed before Him as my Lord so long ago. By now my heart was swimming in His living water. I reveled in His grace and rejoiced in so great a salvation. Then, kneeling at the very place where I first came to Christ, I freshly resolved that I would spend the rest of my life getting what happened to me there to others. The book you're reading is a product of that commitment.

Twenty-five years after my childhood conversion I enrolled in seminary, wanting to learn how to better share this good news that had so radically impacted me. For all its benefits I sometimes struggled while in seminary to keep the gospel on the shelves where anyone could reach it. This wasn't that school's fault; it was my fault. Paul expressed the same concern for the Corinthian believers: "I am afraid that . . . your minds will be led astray from the simplicity and purity of devotion to Christ" (2 Cor. 11:3, NASB).

One day a professor grilled me on the legitimacy of my salvation at such a young age. He was convinced that small children have what he called a "volitional impediment" that prevents them from making monumental, life-altering choices.

"Tell me," the professor quizzed, "that day when you say you were saved, did you understand all the implications of the atonement?"

"No," I replied. "Do you?"

Who among us can scale the heights of God's grace or sound the depths of His love? Thankfully the Bible does not say, "Exegete the gospel and you will be saved." It says, "Believe on the Lord Jesus Christ and you will be saved" (Acts 16:31). The gospel call is clear: "Repent and believe the good news!" (Mark 1:15, NIV).

This journey reminded me again of the why behind our service and devotion. It's easy, even in ministry, to lose sight of the gospel itself. We have been vouchsafed with the greatest Story ever told; we are entrusted with the gospel. This three-stop journey refreshed my inner life and made me feel the comforting tug of steadfast moorings. Once again I felt anchored in the gospel.

The emblem of an anchor served as a very early Christian symbol, even pre-dating signs of a fish or a single cross. Yet this symbolic anchor had a "hidden in plain sight" cross-like construct at the top of the anchor. For the oppressed Christ-followers living under pagan Rome's cruel hand the artful message was clear. The "anchor with a cross" served as something of a code. Living in constant danger because of their faith in Jesus, this symbol reminded these early Christians that their lives were tethered to Christ and His gospel. Their house was built on a solid rock (Matt. 7:24). They had an anchor for their souls (Heb. 6:19).[1]

In our day as storm clouds darken and hatred of the gospel seethes we too must have an anchor with a cross. This book is about anchoring your life in the gospel—prizing it, protecting it, proclaiming it, and living in its priceless privileges. It's a call to put the gospel first—first in our loyalties, first in our preaching, first in how we view people, first in how we view life. If only one of the books I've written lives long beyond my lifetime I pray it will be this book. This book is written for:

- Believers who want to discover (or rediscover) true north in their walk with Christ,

- Multitudes of heartbroken Christians who are leaving church services wondering where the gospel has gone,

- Sincere seekers who would dare to hope that the good news about Jesus really does hold the answers, and

- Today's preachers and coming generations of gospel proclaimers.

I'm writing this book for you. This is the book I had to write. It's the book I had to write now. The acute need for such a book gapes larger by the day. Above all other agendas, followers of Jesus today must cherish and proclaim the gospel as our supreme treasure. If we do not lovingly share the gospel and courageously take a stand for it immediately, it's game over.

The reasons for this book are clear:

Culture is secularizing rapidly. The Western world has cut loose from its biblical moorings and its debt to the gospel. As a result we are adrift in a sea of pluralism where our gospel-laden roots are often disavowed. The notion of a singular way to God is seen by many as intolerant and archaic. The bitter fruit of this dissing of the gospel is a culture that is long on conjectures and short on remedies. Some give in to despair. Others create their own little insulated universe with themselves at the center, only to one day watch their egocentric creation implode. Even as they oppose us, a lost culture is silently pleading with us to call them back to the gospel.

The gospel is being viciously attacked by its enemies. Vitriolic bombasts against the gospel are rising sharply. The Christian faith is routinely pelted by antagonists and parodied by comedians. Wholesale rejection of metanarratives is the norm. The *a priori* judgment is that there surely can't be a "one size fits all" faith for all people at all times in all conditions. Many surmise that ultimate truth is not only unknowable, it just doesn't exist. The greatest love story ever told is being misconstrued as somehow calloused or even cruel.

We have entered the parched wasteland of which Isaiah warns: "Woe to those who call evil good, and good evil; who put darkness for light, and light for darkness; who put bitter for sweet, and sweet for bitter" (Isa. 59:20). Many have traded gold for fool's gold. Yet if we counter their rancor with a vengeful spirit we debase our message and degrade our high calling. Jesus taught us to love our enemies (Matt. 5:44; Luke 6:35). Our response to antagonism must be the love of God expressed in the gospel of Jesus Christ. Christ-haters are daring us to counter their blasphemies. How can we—how dare we—stay silent?

The gospel is being distorted and misrepresented by too many of its proponents. The gospel itself is pristine in its purity. But errors can latch onto the gospel like barnacles. Regrettably, some Christian communicators have sullied the gospel by attaching unsightly parasites. To hear some preachers today, one would think the symbol of our faith is not a cross but a dollar sign. Others equate the gospel with engaging in justice issues, confusing the effects of the gospel with the gospel itself. Some others are like the unscrupulous teachers the Bible describes "who pervert the grace of our God into a license for immorality" (Jude 1:4, NIV). Still others who are well-intentioned assert that there are two gospels—the gospel of salvation and the gospel of the kingdom. The inference is that these two are somehow at odds and that one message is glaringly

...there is only one all-sufficient gospel and its reverberations transform every aspect of life. God's grace is its content, His kingdom is its context.

The screaming need in our day is to again make Jesus Christ and His gospel paramount.

deficient. I will contend in this book that there is only one all-sufficient gospel and its reverberations transform every aspect of life. God's grace is its content, His kingdom is its context. The church has given an uncertain sound regarding this issue. As a result Christ's emissaries are scurrying in multiple directions. What will return us to a cadenced march that will advance the cause of Christ and His purposes in our time? Anchoring our lives—and anchoring the church—in the gospel itself.

The stalwart gospel preachers are moving off the scene. The post-World War II church in America was led by bigger-than-life evangelists. These gospel proclaimers filled stadiums and arenas for decades and saw millions respond to their clear, Christ-centered message. However, these evangelistic giants who kept the gospel front and center are rapidly departing for heaven. Too often we are left with deft communicators who have made lesser agendas their main message. The theme of many today is a me-centered message with no eternal implications. Sadly, *The Four Spiritual Laws* often has been supplanted with "The Seven Steps to Success" and "The Roman Road to Salvation" has been ejected in favor of "Your Path to Personal Fulfillment." Even coating these pep talks with Bible verses cannot cover the nakedness of this cult of self that permeates much of the North American church today.

The screaming need in our day is to again make Jesus Christ and His gospel paramount. Whenever we place anything else center stage it is like rearranging the furniture while the house is on fire! I'm praying this book will help spawn a new generation of Christ-exalting preachers and twenty-first century Gutenbergs who will leverage existing media and build new platforms for gospel proclamation.[2]

Young people are confused but searching. Studies show that even many teenagers raised in evangelical churches who say they are Christians actually espouse a "moralistic, therapeutic deism."[3]

This feel-good smörgåsbord theology can run directly counter to the gospel. The upshot is that while the biblical gospel is often derided on campuses a nebulous spirituality is considered cool. Without the objective plumb line of the gospel of Jesus Christ, today's autonomous, self-styled religions can be summed up in the stinging critique, "Everyone did what was right in his own eyes" (Judg. 17:6).

In the midst of this arid spiritual wilderness vast numbers of people languish for living water (John 4:10). They're desperately seeking God, though they often mask their search with sedatives of drugs, sex, incessant entertainment, or a zombie-like escapism. Though culture constantly tells them truth is unknowable their heart tells them something else. Somehow they just know there is ultimate good and a Creator-God who bestows all good things. Deep inside they are sure there are eternal verities. This book will point true inquirers to the one and only door that opens to flourishing, forever life. Jesus said, "I am the door. If anyone enters by Me, he will be saved" (John 10:9).

The gospel is the one message above all others I owe this generation and generations to come. This book seeks to honor Christ, exult in His finished work, and markedly raise the profile of the gospel. When Jesus is lifted up people are attracted to Him (John 12:22).

But His gospel also repels. When the call to forsake all and follow Jesus is issued it is the aroma of life for some and the stench of death for others (2 Cor. 2:15-16). Jesus said that His way is a narrow road (Matt. 7:13-14). Still, the most basic of all human rights is the right of everyone everywhere to hear the gospel. Reception of the gospel lifts people to their full potential and dignity.

Through this book I pray that the gospel will be clarified, believers will be edified, and Jesus will be glorified. May this book find its way into the hands of tens of thousands of pastors, church leaders, seminarians, and hungry Christians who long to see the gospel exhibited as our highest treasure and our supreme gift to the world.

In addressing a subject as vast and sublime as the gospel of Jesus

Christ I cry out with Paul, "Who is sufficient for these things?" (2 Cor. 2:16). I've felt my limitations more acutely in writing this book than any project I've ever tackled. I'm keenly aware that the Holy Spirit must breathe God's life into this work for it to benefit anyone. But I'm also heartened by the promise, "Our sufficiency is from God, who also made us sufficient as ministers of the new covenant, not of the letter but of the Spirit" (2 Cor. 3:5-6).

Jesus Christ "has abolished death and brought life and immortality to light through the gospel" (2 Tim. 1:10). In an age of virulent belligerence against it, we have been given custody of the best news the world will ever hear. Its message gushes with light, life, and hope. This is our time. This is our call. We're entrusted with the gospel. Let's make it the anchor of our lives.

— David Shibley

ONE

THE GOSPEL—
CLEAR ON ITS CONTENT

Now brothers, I want to clarify for you the gospel I proclaimed to you; you received it and have taken your stand on it. You are also saved by it, if you hold to the message I proclaimed to you—unless you believed for no purpose. For I passed on to you as most important what I also received: that Christ died for our sins according to the Scriptures, that He was buried, that He was raised on the third day according to the Scriptures.

1 Cor. 15:1-4, HCSB

The gospel is not just supposed to be our ticket into heaven; it is to be an entirely new basis for how we relate to God, ourselves, and others. It is to be the source from which everything else flows.

— J. D. Greear
Gospel: Recovering the Power that Made Christianity Revolutionary

The gospel is the game-changer.

No other message has such explosive, transforming qualities. When the gospel and the searching heart link something so life-altering takes place Jesus described it as a new birth, being born a second time (John 3:3-8). The gospel literally gives us another shot at life.

Just ask a London teenager named Charles. Though Charles was raised in a churchgoing family he was a young man in deep turmoil of soul, gripped by guilt and anxiety. Peace eluded him. Desperate to find an answer this young seeker braved a blizzard to get to church, and hopefully get to God and peace.

Unable to reach the church he usually attended because of the severe weather, fifteen-year-old Charles ducked into a small Primitive Methodist chapel. There were just eight people in attendance, all huddled around a coal burning stove. The bitter conditions had even kept the pastor away. But a simple, short unpacking of the best news Charles had ever heard would soon be delivered by an unsung hero.

In the pastor's absence a "swarthy faced and grimy handed blacksmith" stood to speak. He read Isaiah 45:22, "Look to Me, and be saved, all you ends of the earth!" Pointing his bony finger at the anguished young man he cried, "Look, young man! Look! Look to Christ!"

That pivotal night Charles heard the gist of the gospel: Look away from yourself. Look away from your sin. Look to Christ! Look and live! (Num. 21:4-9; John 3:14-16). And on that snowy night young Charles Spurgeon looked in faith to God's crucified, risen Son. He later testified, "I could dance all the way home. . . . As the snow fell on my road home . . . I thought every snowflake talked with me and told of the pardon I had found."[1]

The nameless smithy is a footnote in history but he is well known in heaven. The one convert from that blacksmith's one short sermon soon started preaching himself to throngs of people. Charles Spurgeon's gospel-anchored ministry shook London and the world for the next four decades. Even today he is recognized as one of the most prolific and most quoted communicators in the church's history. And it all began with a simple proclamation of the gospel, wrapped in a few words from an untrained, Jesus-loving blacksmith who knew he was entrusted with God's remedy for sin.

Stories like this are replicated every day. Such is the power of this good news. Yes, the gospel changes everything. I know.

The gospel changed everything for me. Its message has rocked and reshaped my world. And now the God behind the gospel is so mightily at work in my life that eventually I will be like Jesus (1 John 3:2). This is not hubris on my part. It's His promise (Ro. 8:28-29). God alone will do this because of the gospel alone.

My colossal assignment in this book is to make the unfathomable simple. Yet this is precisely what God has done in His message to the world. While the gospel is by no means simplistic, it is simple. If I were sharing The Big Story with someone completely unfamiliar with its message I would say something like this:

We were all far away from God because we all chose to walk away from His love and His ways. We went our own way instead of God's way so we all walked into darkness. With every step away from God it drew darker. No one could find the way back to God. But God loved us still and sent Jesus, His Son, to shine the light to the world and bring us back to God. Only Jesus always went God's way and only Jesus can bring us back to God. Going our own way instead of God's way is sin; we've all done it. Jesus paid for every step we've made away from God when He died for us on the cross. When He died He took all our darkness and offered us all His light. Three days later He broke out of death and now He is alive forever. Now He offers this same forever life to us. Without Jesus we would have forever been in the dark, without God and without hope. But when we turn around and go God's way and trust Jesus to take us out of darkness we become brand new. Jesus puts His light and life in us! It's just like being born a second time. Jesus brings us light and a new life.

This is the good news we want to tell everyone, everywhere! No scholar can sound its depths yet a child can grasp its truth. In fact, children often comprehend the gospel essence more readily than many adults. Skepticism and speculation don't get in the way. No wonder Jesus taught that to enter His kingdom we must become as children (Matt. 18:3). The nine-year-olds in any Bible-believing church should have a clear grasp of the crux of the gospel or somebody isn't doing his job.

I was a privileged child, not financially but spiritually. I got the gospel early. Not only did I hear it, I got it. One of my first encounters with the gospel was through the four colorful pages of what is aptly titled, *The Wordless Book*.[2] This little book is comprised of just four pages. Its only printed content is colors. No words, just colors. The dark page points to the darkness of our defiance of God and His ways. The red page tells of Jesus' payment for our sins with His blood. The clean page reminds us that we are made new when we receive His cleansing. The gold page assures us of a home with Him forever in heaven. The cover is green, encouraging us to be ever-growing in our walk with the Lord. There it is—the beauty of the gospel, pure and simple.

The concept for *The Wordless Book* came (not surprisingly) from the mind and heart of Charles Spurgeon. Having responded to a lucid unfolding of the gospel himself, Spurgeon now determined to get God's good news to many more children—including the disenfranchised and illiterate. Hence, *The Wordless Book* was born.[3]

Almost a century later Francis Roberts, a director with Child Evangelism Fellowship in the 1940s, penned a simple song to describe the little book's good news. Wanting to keep the core of the gospel clear for even small children she wrote,

My heart was dark with sin until the
Savior came in; [dark page]
His precious blood, I know, [red page]
Has washed me white as snow. [clean page]
And in His Word I'm told I'll walk the streets of gold. [gold page]
Oh, wonderful, wonderful day;
He washed my sins away!

Don't tell me you can't make profound theology clear. The great preacher Vance Havner observed, "It's about time we gave up all this theological grand opera and went back to practicing the scales."[4] This book is a call to go back and practice the scales. Let the gospel recalibrate your life and give your heart a thorough tune-up. All the majestic hymns of redemption are but a rearranging of the simple notes of salvation's sweet song.

The world grows more complex by the day. Think about it. When televisions first came out folks just plugged the cord in the socket and selected from three snowy-screened channels that were transmitting in real time. Today it seems a tech wizard is required to wire our intricate media systems. The fuzzy black and white pictures have given way to brilliant colors in high definition. And the three original choices have mushroomed into access to hundreds of channels, satellite radio, movies, and games on demand—all coming out of our television—or smart phone, or computer, or iPad, to mention just a few delivery systems. And for our "convenience" all of this input can be paused, recorded, or played live. This is but one indicator of an age where more options also means more complexity.

Into this confusing, chaotic, creative time one pristine, timeless message endures—unchanged, unvarnished, unrivaled, unhindered. Not only will it change your life, it will anchor your life. It is the forthright message of the gospel of Jesus Christ.

THE NEED FOR THE GOSPEL

When we view our broken world we might tend to think it was always this way. But God created a perfect world. Earth's first human inhabitants were placed in a perfect environment. They walked with God, enjoyed His presence, and exhibited His nature. But a germ of defiance against God and His ways was placed in their hearts by the devil. Willfully going against

God's clear commands (directives He had given only for their good) Adam and Eve chose their own way over God's. From that moment all mankind—and his habitat—began to die (Gen. 3:1-14). This willful choice to go against God, His word, and His ways is the essence of sin.

But ever since man's rebellion against Him, God has been on a rescue mission of love to recover what was lost. God's relentless love has always characterized His dealings with humanity. After their sin Adam and Eve experienced the natural consequence of their rebellion, a desire to hide from God. But the Father-heart of God came calling. God employed an aggressive "evangelistic" strategy as He lovingly forced our first parents to face their sin. From the moment humankind's fellowship with their Creator was broken, God has been in the business of restoring it. In the same breath that God pronounced judgment on man's rebellion He also promised a redeemer (Gen. 3:15). This *protoevangelium* (first gospel) brought hope for restored communion with God and for a restored world. Sin's consequence was a curse on all humanity and on creation itself. Sin's cure would come through a mighty Savior—the "seed of the woman," Jesus Christ—who would break sin's curse by taking the curse upon Himself (Gal. 3:13-14).

Sin never merely affects the one who sins. Sin always has lamentable ramifications for others. When Adam chose his own way instead of God's, all humanity was adversely impacted. Adam's sin affected, indeed infected, every human life. "Through one man sin entered into the world, and death through sin, and thus death spread to all men, because all sinned" (Ro. 5:12). You and I have inherited what theologians call the Adamic nature—a bent toward defiance against God and His ways. Yet in the midst of mankind's rebellion God was weaving a story of breathtaking reconciliation.

For the expressed purpose of showering His mercy on all the peoples of the earth, God called out a man named Abram. God covenanted to bless him, again for a specific purpose. "Get out of your country," God told him, "from your family and from your father's house, to a land that I will show you. I will make you a great nation; I will bless you and make your name great; and you shall be a blessing—and in you all the families of the earth shall be blessed (Gen. 12:1-3)."

From Abram (later named Abraham) a seed came that would bring universal blessing. The Bible is clear that this seed of blessing is Jesus Christ. But Christ came in human flesh through a specific line of faith, from Abraham. This line of faith from which the Messiah appeared continued through Abraham's son, Isaac.

From Isaac a nation was born. This nation was to bear God's light and truth to all peoples. A very clear commission was given to God's ancient people: "Declare His glory among the nations, His wonders among all peoples" (Ps. 96:3). Far from being a tribal deity of the Hebrews, God declared His intention to be worshiped for who He is—King over all His creation. The ancient people of Israel were to be God's agents to bring all nations and peoples to worship Him.

Somewhere along the line, however, the carriers of God's message distorted their commission. They began to view other ethnicities with suspicion and even hatred. Instead of being a light to surrounding nations, God's ancient people became riddled with provincialism, ethnic pride, and a protectionist mentality.

A new covenant between God and people was established through Jesus Christ. Under this new covenant, the children of God are those who receive His Son and believe on His name for salvation (John 1:12). The story reaches its climax in God's stunning love-display when He personally smashed our sins on His Son (Isa. 53:6). This transfer of guilt was literally earth-shaking. The creation itself quaked in revulsion and daytime shut off the light as the sinless Savior absorbed all our sin. When

Jesus' body was torn for us, the curtain barrier in the Temple separating God's holy presence from unholy people was also ripped, from top to bottom. It was an unmistakable visual aid to help us comprehend what had just transpired (Matt. 27:51).

No more separation! No more searching for God and not finding Him! Now the way to God, long barricaded by rebellion and even religion, carries a joy-filled invitation: Access granted! Now without shame or fear we can walk into the very control center of the universe "by the blood of Jesus, by a new and living way which He consecrated for us, through the veil, that is, His flesh" (Heb. 10:19-20). No wonder Oswald Chambers wrote, "The cross is the center of Time and Eternity, the answer to the enigmas of both."[5]

Three days later Jesus stood up—pulsating with God's life, triumphant over death! God broke into time in Christ's incarnation. Thus the closed system of naturalism was negated. God broke through the rift between His creation and Himself by bridging the gap through His Son's atonement on the cross. Now God breaks through life's impossibilities by His Son's resurrection! And with His resurrection our way of seeing broadens and brightens. Death no longer gets the final word. Now all things are possible. God can do anything. He brings the dead to life! This is the rock-solid, anchored hope of the gospel!

God's Remedy through the Gospel

The Bible's integrating theme is this awesome story of how God Himself intervened to save His fallen creation, hell-bent on self-destruction. A scarlet thread of redemption weaves God's story together. Redemption means "to purchase again." Jesus has purchased us. The method of payment was His own blood. He has redeemed us back to God by fully paying the price to spring us from Satan's trap.

Because of man's rebellion against God, Satan wreaked havoc over humanity. Romans 6:23 says, "The wages of sin is death,"—physically, spiritually, and culturally. In His immense mercy, God intervened through Jesus Christ and stripped Satan of all authority. By legal right, Jesus Christ is now ruler over this planet. "For by Him all things were created that are in heaven and that are on earth, whether thrones or dominions or principalities or powers. All things were created through Him and for Him" (Col. 1:16).

The Gospels are four narratives by four of Christ's disciples regarding His life, death, resurrection, ascension and promised return. In Matthew the "gospel of the kingdom" is announced. Mark and Luke refer more to this good news simply as "the gospel." The other New Testament writers draw out implications and applications of this good news. What the Old Testament prophets had hoped for and seen (if only partially) through the eyes of faith was now breaking into history with clarity. God's righteousness and rule were now being revealed. This new covenant and new kingdom center in King Jesus. One day all creation will see the coronation and exaltation of Christ as King. His rule over everything was guaranteed by an event that seemed at the time to be a defeat—Christ's captors crucified Him. What eluded their grasp however was that His death and resurrection would authorize and jump start His reign over everything, everywhere. The gospel of the kingdom and the gospel of grace are the same good news: Jesus died and made the payment for our sins. He rose as rightful Lord of all of life. He reigns over all. Everything—that's right, *everything*—will one day find its consummation in Jesus Christ. We will forever be wrapped up in Him.[6]

A scarlet thread of redemption weaves God's story together.

This book's focus is on God's redemption of fallen people. Therefore, the gospel

> The gospel of the kingdom and the gospel of grace are the same good news: Jesus died and made the payment for our sins. He rose as rightful Lord of all of life. He reigns over all.

emphasis in these pages is more God, man, Christ, response. However, the more narrative form of the gospel—creation, fall, redemption, restoration—which emphasizes the restoration of a marred creation is also vitally important. "For God has allowed us to know the secret of his plan, and it is this: he purposed long ago in his sovereign will that all human history shall be consummated in Christ; that everything that exists in Heaven or earth shall find its perfection and fulfillment in him." (Eph. 1:10, Phillips). Because of Jesus, we are headed for new heavens and a new earth (2 Pet. 3:13). So look up! Your redemption (and creation's redemption) is at hand (Luke 21:28).

Amazing Grace

What adjective is sufficient to describe God's favor toward us, His work on our behalf, and His enablement in our lives? Scan the dictionary and one of the best of admittedly limited options we have to more fully describe God's grace is—it's just amazing.

Most religions teach moral rectitude. But what separates Christianity from all other religions is our message—this good news of salvation and restoration through Jesus. The gospel announces the joyful news that righteousness is not man's achievement. Rather, God's own righteousness is placed on us and in us through Christ's redeeming work. As a result believers are loosed into "the glorious liberty of the children of God" (Ro.

8:21). It is primarily through proclamation and reception of this message that individuals and nations are reborn.

In the Bible, the main things are the plain things and the plain things are the main things. Both the Bible's foes and friends agree there are subjects in the Scriptures that challenge the intellect and are hard to understand. But the gospel is not one of those subjects. The gospel is clear. However, it takes the revealing ministry of the Holy Spirit for hearts and minds darkened by sin to truly comprehend it. What sets the gospel apart from the messages of other religions is its uniqueness. Unique aspects of God's good news include:

- *God's grace.* The good news of the gospel is that God takes the initiative to close the gap between rebellious humanity and Himself. While grace includes mercy it is much more, as we will see. With no prerequisite of our own goodness or merit God receives us because our transgressions against Him have been paid for by Christ. "For by grace you have been saved through faith; and that not of yourselves; it is the gift of God" (Eph. 2:8).

- *God's righteousness.* All other religions essentially lay out requirements necessary to appease some deity and gain right standing with that deity by one's own works and merit. But in the gospel God's righteousness—not ours—is both put in us and put on our account. "In the gospel the righteousness of God is revealed—a righteousness that is by faith from first to last" (Ro. 1:17, NIV).

- *Christ's death in our place.* This is what theologians call substitutionary atonement. We deserved to be sentenced to death and separation. Our willful rebellion against Him made us fully deserving of God's wrath and judgment. Jesus intervened and absorbed the judgment we should have endured; He stood in as our substitute. His blood was the sacrifice God accepted to remove our guilt. "When we were still powerless, Christ died for the ungodly . . . God demonstrates His own love for us in this: While we were still sinners, Christ died for us" (Ro. 5:6-8).

- *Christ's resurrection.* When Jesus broke out of that tomb it was God's stamp of approval on His sacrifice. It verified all His claims to deity and lordship. "But now Christ is risen from the dead, and has become the first-fruits of those who have fallen asleep" (1 Cor. 15:20). The resurrection dramatically displays Christ's triumph over the kingdom of darkness, and even death itself. His resurrection ensures the future restoration of all creation. "I am the Living One," Jesus declares, "and now look, I am alive for ever and ever. And I hold the keys of death and Hades" (Rev. 1:18, NIV).

- *A restored creation.* Paul wrote that "the whole creation groans and labors with birth pangs together until now" (Ro. 8:22). All the painful convulsions of nature are creation's ways of crying out for a new birth of order and tranquility. The gospel brings the sure hope that this will surely come. "We, according to His promise, look for new heavens and a new earth in which righteousness dwells" (2 Pet. 3:13). The restoration of Earth itself is tied to a revelation of the sons of God—those who have been transformed by Jesus Christ and His gospel (Ro. 8:19-22).

The gospel is indeed the game-changer. Grace is God at work for us. God has acted decisively and dramatically to bring us back to Him. The Creator became part of His own creation in the person of His Son, Jesus Christ. This perfect God-Man took our sin, guilt, and shame. In exchange for our sin He gives us His righteousness. As the first to break death's grip Jesus offers fabulous and forever life with Him to all who look in faith to Him, turning from their shortcomings to His sufficiency.

Defining the Gospel

The heart of the gospel is also the hope of the gospel. The infinite, transcendent God personally intervened by His grace in our helpless, hopeless condition when we were severed from Him by our rebellion. In love He sent His eternal Son to become a man and pay for our defiance through the perfect sacrifice of His blood. Now, risen and reigning, Jesus offers pardon and eternal life to all who will turn in faith from their sin to His salvation, from their rebellion to His rule, from their futile attempts at self-righteousness to the free gift of His righteousness.

The Greek word *euangelion* which is translated *gospel* appears 76 times in the New Testament. New Testament writers describe it as the gospel of the kingdom, the gospel of the grace of God, the gospel of Christ, the gospel of God and most often simply as the gospel. It is the underpinning of all of Scripture, the skeletal structure of the entire biblical witness. The gospel is the good news about the salvation God has provided through Jesus Christ. The gospel is "the power of God for the salvation of everyone who believes" (Ro. 1:16). The gospel also speaks to the fulfillment of the Old Testament promise of the current and coming kingdom of God (Mark 1:15).

"The greatest idea in history, the one that has produced the most significant and enduring benefit to humanity, is Jesus Christ," writes Rice Broocks. "God's idea to come to earth as a human, undeniably demonstrating the power of truth, has given us the ultimate message of hope, called the gospel or good news. . . . The good news announces that God became man in Jesus Christ, He lived the life we should have lived, and in our place He died the death we should have died. Three days later He came back

> This is the gospel—the ultimate good news! Above all other agendas it is our privilege, honor, and duty to give the gospel the widest possible audience in our own generation, then deliver it intact to the next generation.

to life to verify His identity as the Son of God, and now He offers pardon and forgiveness to all who will believe and turn from the darkness of sin and the futility of trying to save themselves. Those who turn and put their trust in Him will never be ashamed."[7]

Ed Stetzer describes the gospel as "the good news that God, who is more holy than we can imagine, looked upon with compassion, people, who are more sinful than we would possibly admit, and sent Jesus into history to establish His Kingdom and reconcile people and the world to Himself. Jesus, whose love is more extravagant than we can measure, came to sacrificially die for us so that, by his death and resurrection, we might gain through His grace what the Bible defines as new and eternal life."[8]

Ché Ahn depicts the gospel message as "the stunning story of what Jesus has done for us. It is a faithful recounting of how Jesus willingly took our place and died for our sins. It is testimony to the fact that He sacrificed His life for us on the cross to make us right with God in the only way possible as the perfect sacrifice. It is the promise of the forgiveness of sins and the gift of eternal life to all who repent and believe."[9]

This is the gospel—the ultimate good news! Above all other agendas it is our privilege, honor, and duty to give the gospel the widest possible audience in our own generation, then deliver it intact to the next generation. "The most important baton we pass to the next generation is the gospel of Jesus Christ," writes Steve Murrell. "If we drop the gospel baton or leave it at the starting line, everything else we do in ministry is a waste of time."[10] What a stewardship we've been given! "God was pleased to trust us with his message" (1 Thess. 2:4, CEV). Astounding.

THE WEEKEND THAT CHANGED THE WORLD

What must it have been like to be the apostle John, watching Jesus ensure the care of His mother even as He secured the redemption of the world? What must have raced through Peter's heart as he sprinted toward Jesus' tomb to verify the report that the body was gone and the Roman guard were nowhere in sight?

In these eternally pivotal events—Christ's cross and His resurrection—every religious myth is exposed and exploded. Through His death Jesus blasted through the sin barrier that held people at bay from God. Through His resurrection He abolished death itself. It is God's power-packed one-two punch that deals the death blow to all of hell's schemes for humanity—and for you.

This hub of history—the God-Man's death and defiance of death—is also the apex of history. "Love crucified arose!"[11] Our sacrificed Savior is forever our living Lord. This composite saving act of God in history changes everything. All our hopes are rooted in these two historically verifiable acts which comprise God's completed saving activity. Henry Blackaby is right: "God always connects the cross with the resurrection. This is true in His plan and purpose, and must be true in our own thinking as well, because there's no victory over sin without the resurrection. . . . On the cross, Jesus Christ in His body carried the weight of the sin of the world; but not until three days later, when He rose bodily from the dead, was God's plan of salvation complete. The resurrection confirmed it: The sacrifice had been accepted! Sin had been dealt with decisively, and the unsurpassable evidence of that fact was the risen, living body of the Lord Jesus."[12]

When Jesus burst out of that tomb, your destiny and mine

took a sharp turn upward. Our chains fell off! Death no longer gets the final word. His resurrection guarantees ours. "Because I live," Jesus promised, "you will live also" (John 14:19).

REDEEMING LOVE

As a young boy who responded to Jesus' call I thought, "There's nothing like the gospel." As a broken-hearted teenager whose dad had just died I realized, "Nothing brings hope like the gospel." Through college and seminary as I surveyed the world's philosophies and religions I saw even more clearly that nothing compares to the gospel. As a young preacher with high hopes and vast vision my heart pulsated, "Nothing calls for my allegiance like the gospel." In mid-life as pressures mounted and mocked me I recognized once again, "There's nothing like the gospel." Now in my sixties as long-standing friends are dying and mortality shoves me toward eternity, I am more convinced than ever—there's nothing like the gospel.

That's why, along with the unnamed messenger in Second Corinthians, I want to be so drenched, so anchored in this good news that I too may be known as "the brother whose praise is in the gospel" (2 Cor. 8:18).

I love to tell the story of unseen things above,
Of Jesus and His glory, of Jesus and His love.
I love to tell the story because I know 'tis true;
It satisfies my longing as nothing else can do.

I love to tell the story for those who know it best
Seem hungering and thirsting to hear it like the rest.
And when, in scenes of glory, I sing the new, new song,
'Twill be the old, old story that I have loved so long.[13]

This old, old story is ever new. It's timeless. It is relevant to every generation, every culture, every person. The eminent Bible expositor, Martyn Lloyd-Jones, described the gospel as "the most interesting, the most thrilling, the most absorbing subject in the universe."[14] No wonder even angels are fixated and fascinated by the gospel. This matchless message vouchsafes "things which angels desire to look into" (1 Pet. 1:12). Jared Wilson writes that the gospel "is fascinating! It is eternally interesting. It is thrilling. It is simple, yet complex. It is a diamond: one brilliant treasure with a million gleaming facets, each offering a million vantage points alight and gleaming with the majesty of its architect."[15]

One faith-filled look at Jesus transformed Charles Spurgeon's life when he was a teenager starved for answers and desperate for peace. He would pour the rest of his life into rolling out the glories of the gospel, employing his stellar skills to at least try to do justice to its magnificence. The church Spurgeon served as pastor for many years is London's Metropolitan Tabernacle. Today, walking into that church's auditorium you see these words from Isaiah 45:22 beautifully emblazoned above the baptistry:

"LOOK UNTO ME, AND BE YE SAVED,
ALL THE ENDS OF THE EARTH."

Spurgeon never got over God's grace. What captured his heart that wintry night consumed him throughout his life. So let's make one more stop in London—Spurgeon's tomb. Let's pause a moment and thank God for a life forever changed by the gospel and for the millions who have been introduced to the gospel and its glories through his witness.

As we walk to the side of the tomb we read four lines from yet another gospel hymn. They sum up Spurgeon. They tell his story in the far bigger drama that is His Story:

ENTRUSTED

E'er since by faith I saw the stream
Thy flowing wounds supply,
Redeeming love has been my theme,
And shall be 'til I die.[16]

This story of redeeming love is the best news you'll ever hear. And the awesome attraction of this matchless message is a peerless person.

TWO

THE GOSPEL—
CAPTURED BY ITS SUBJECT

In this the love of God was manifested toward us, that God has sent His only begotten Son into the world, that we might live through Him.

1 John 4:9

Who is this who spreads the victory feast?
Who is this who makes our warring cease?
Jesus, risen Savior, Prince of Peace!
God and Man at table are sat down.

Robert Stamps
God and Man at Table are Sat Down

It's all about Jesus.

The star of this story is Jesus Christ. Paul said that the gospel is "concerning His Son, Jesus Christ our Lord" (Ro. 1:3). In His life He is humanity's only perfection; in His death, humanity's only Savior; in His resurrection, humanity's only hope.

Yes, we are the objects of His love, but the subject of the gospel is Jesus. Let's not confuse the object with the subject. Our personal salvation stories are not the gospel; they are testimonies to the power of the gospel. We're not saved merely because we gave our

...we are the objects of His love, but the subject of the gospel is Jesus. Let's not confuse the object with the subject.

lives to Jesus; we are saved because Jesus gave His life for us. The gospel is not first about you. Or me. It's about Jesus, the soul-saving, death-destroying, life-giving, freedom-granting, kingdom-conquering, eternal Son of God.

Ed Stetzer writes, "Jesus isn't just part of the Bible story, He is the point of the Bible story. . . . I believe that interpreting God's word must be mediated through Jesus Christ. He is the lens through which we see the Scriptures. . . . every story casts His shadow. Every word, every verse is His testimony—the holy Messiah. Jesus Christ. Eternal King."[1]

John Wesley, the founder of Methodism, returned late one night from a preaching assignment. His brother, Charles, inquired as to the subject of John's sermon that night. "What did you give the people?" Charles asked. John Wesley replied, "I gave them Christ."

That is my hope and assignment for this chapter. Jesus Christ— God in flesh, mighty to save, King over all, Savior of all who look in faith to Him—He is the subject of the gospel. May we be so captured by Him that we can affirm with Paul, "Christ, who is our life" (Col. 3:4).

GOD IN FLESH

For me, the greatest miracle in history is the Incarnation. "God contracted to a span," as Charles Wesley extolled, "incomprehensibly made man."[2] His birth births infinite possibilities and undiluted hope. If the Creator-God has broken into time and space, this spawns a whole new way of viewing life:

All things are possible. God can intervene in your life!

Jesus is God in flesh. All His other attributes both as God and Man flow from this assertion. This one born of a virgin (the only one so born) has unique powers and a unique qualification. He is, as one tuned-in child described Him, "God with skin on." This God with skin on is the only one capable of spanning the chasm between the holy Creator-God and His rebellious creation, humankind. And He did it! His cross became the bridge that brings God and man together. Jesus has mediated an end of God's holy wrath against sin by taking our sin on Himself. And it all began when love found a way—in a manger.

In a real sense, the gospel took root in our world that holy night. The angel of the Lord announced to the amazed shepherds, "I bring you good tidings of great joy which will be to all people. For there is born to you this day in the city of David a Savior, who is Christ the Lord" (Lu. 2:10). The word in the original Greek, euangellizomai, can literally be translated, "I proclaim the gospel of great joy . . ." This joyful announcement, though brief, brings great revelation as to who this baby is—He is the Savior, the Messiah, the Lord. The scope of the gospel is also declared – this Good News is to be "to all people."

I've always appreciated the ability of the best lyricists to encapsulate profound truths in a few choice words. Graham Kendrick did this as well as any composer of our time on the topic of the Incarnation when he wrote,

Wisdom unsearchable
God the invisible
Love indestructible
In frailty appears.
Lord of infinity
Stooping so tenderly
Lifts our humanity
To the heights of His throne.

41

O what a mystery
Meekness and majesty
Bow down and worship
For this is your God.[3]

To be clear on what the gospel is, we must be clear on who Jesus is. There is unquestionably a uniqueness about Jesus. Meekness and majesty are conjoined in Him. Let's delve deeper into the person and redeeming work of Jesus of Nazareth, God in flesh.

WHO HE IS

Of all who have ever lived, there is simply no one like Jesus. There's a reason for that—He is the uniquely born, eternal Son of God, "Very God of Very God," as stated in The Nicene Creed. Theologian F. F. Bruce observed, "That one Who had His being eternally within the unity of the Godhead became man at a point in time, without relinquishing His oneness with God."[4]

No wonder Jesus has always been captivating—not only to His followers, but to the entire world. Some three hundred years ago a young, wealthy man named Nikolaus von Zinzendorf was touring one of Europe's great art galleries. As he observed many masterpieces suddenly he was transfixed by Domenico Feti's magnificent painting, *Ecce Homo* (Latin for *Behold the Man*, Jn. 19:5). As Zinzendorf gazed at the painting the Lord spoke to His heart, "This have I done for you; now what will you do for Me?"[5] Gripped by Christ's sacrifice for him, Zinzendorf determined to show his gratitude by advancing the gospel message. He gave refuge on his large estate to serious-minded missionaries called the Moravians and gave spiritual direction to what became one of the strongest world mission movements in church history. It all began with an enthralled look at Jesus.

Sadly, instead of gazing on Jesus, people today are messing with Him. Many try to leverage Him for their agendas, soften

His demands, strip Him of His deity, or make Him cool for contemporary culture. He is caricatured as everything from a heartless demagogue to a mystical pundit to a social radical. Jesus has been labeled everything from a flag-waving capitalist to a flag-burning anarchist. These contortions of the peerless God-Man range from humorous to nauseating.

But to discover the truth about Him we must return to the only fully reliable source, the holy Scriptures of the Old and New Testaments. Entire libraries could be written (and have been written) on the isolated subject of Christology, the study of the person and work of Jesus Christ. Here we are limited to a short summary.

Jesus Himself claimed to be divine. He said, "I and the Father are one" (Jn. 10:30). When interrogated by the high priest He was specifically questioned, "Tell us if you are the Christ, the Son of God." Jesus responded, "Yes, it is as you say" (Matt. 26:63-64). The Jews understood very clearly what Jesus was claiming about Himself. That's why He was charged with blasphemy and why they were determined to kill Him (Jn. 5:18).

The noted Presbyterian missionary, Robert Speer, observed, "The sinlessness of Jesus and His assurance and consciousness of this sinlessness constitute a fact so lonely and unmatched that it must be set down by itself. He shows no consciousness at any time of any moral failure or of any feeling of need for personal repentance and forgiveness."[6] As the perfect God-Man He alone is in a position to atone for our sin.

As the eternal God, He displayed and displays authority—over everything. Depending on your understanding of who Jesus truly is, this pronouncement He made is either the most audacious or most compelling decree in history: "All authority has been given to Me in heaven and on earth" (Matt. 28:18). He exercises authority over nature (Mk. 4:39; Jn. 2:7-11); disease (Mk. 3:10); demons (Lu. 4:35); and death itself (Jn. 11:43-44). Death could not hold Him. He has destroyed its power (Heb. 2:14-15).

Jesus Christ is so fully in charge that the decree from God the Father is that the final judgment of the world will be consigned to God the Son (Jn. 5:26-27; Ac. 17:30-31). As God, Jesus is the pre-existent One (Jn. 8:57-58). He is both creator and sustainer of everything (Jn. 1:3, Col. 1:17). Among His attributes as God, He is omniscient (Mk. 2:8; Jn. 2:25) and omnipotent (Heb. 1:3). He is the very icon of God almighty (Jn. 1:1; Col. 1:15).

The eternal God took on human flesh in Jesus Christ. "In Him dwells all the fullness of the Godhead bodily" (Col.2:9). He was worshiped by His disciples and He accepted their worship. Peter's confession of faith was, "You have the words of eternal life. Also we have come to believe and know that You are the Christ, the Son of the living God" (Jn. 6:68-69). When Thomas encountered the resurrected Christ, he exclaimed, "My lord and my God!" (Jn. 20:28).

Yet God incarnate voluntarily emptied Himself of certain prerogatives of deity. In his famous *kenosis* (emptying) passage, Paul tells us, "Christ Jesus, who, existing in the form of God, did not consider equality with God as something to be used for His own advantage. Instead, He emptied Himself by assuming the form of a slave, taking on the likeness of men. And when He had come as a man in His external form, He humbled Himself by becoming obedient to the point of death—even to death on a cross. For this reason God highly exalted Him and gave Him the name that is above every name, so that at the name of Jesus every knee will bow—of those who are in heaven and on earth and under the earth—and every tongue should confess that Jesus Christ is Lord, to the glory of God the Father" (Phil. 2:5-11, HCSB).

To the apostle Paul, as to any devout Jew, "the name that is above every name" could refer only to the Jews' sacred name of God, the sacred tetragrammaton which is transliterated in English as *Jehovah* or *Yahweh*. This name was so exalted and set apart that reverential Jews were forbidden even to pronounce it. But now Paul says that this name—this name above all names—

belongs to Jesus. He is Messiah; He is Lord over all!

In 451 A.D. The Council of Chalcedon succinctly summed up the orthodox view of the uniqueness of the person and nature of Jesus Christ:

1. There are two natures; a human nature and a divine nature.
2. Each nature has its completeness and integrity.
3. These two natures are organically and indissolubly united, so no third nature is formed thereby.
4. Orthodox doctrine forbids us either to divide the person or confound the natures.[7]

God became man in the person of Jesus, the Messiah. Jesus is the Son of God, but He is also God, the Son. Now He "has gone into heaven and is at the right hand of God, angels and authorities and powers having been made subject to Him" (1 Pet.3:22).

The uniqueness of Jesus as God in flesh is at the very core of our message and therefore our mission. Who is Jesus and what will you do with Him? This is the Great Divide, the all-important question.

WHY HE CAME

Almost every religion has high regard for Jesus. But whether or not He is the one and only redeemer—or if people even need a redeemer—is where biblical Christianity parts company with every other faith. Who Jesus is and what His cross is all about is the central abrasive issue. David Platt reminds us, "He was not a coward about to face Roman soldiers. Instead, he was a Savior about to endure divine wrath."[8]

This cross—this sacrifice—that is so repugnant to others is attractive and precious to us who believe. It is at the same time the ultimate tragedy and the ultimate triumph. Beth Moore writes, "God had crossed days off the kingdom calendar, preparing heaven and earth for this one. The worst and the best day of all."[9]

Here is the testimony of Jesus Himself as to why He left the splendor of heaven for the squalor of earth: "The Son of Man has come to seek and to save that which was lost" (Lu. 19:10). Add to this, the testimony of the apostles. Paul declared, "Christ Jesus came into the world to save sinners" (1 Tim. 1:15). John asserted, "For this purpose the Son of God was manifested, that He might destroy the works of the devil" (1 Jn. 3:8).

To use the theological term, He came to make atonement for our sins. He has restored our relationship with God, which was severed by our rebellion. Now we are in a standing of "at-one-ment" with God. "We rejoice in God through our Lord Jesus Christ, through whom we have now received the reconciliation" (Ro. 5:11).

Beginning with the church's first theologians, men have tried to unpack the profundity of this greatest of all transactions. Some explain that Jesus' death provided a ransom to free us from sin, Satan, and ultimately from death itself. Jesus came to "give His life a ransom for many" (Matt. 20:28). Related to this is the *Christus Victor* viewpoint that stresses Christ's victory over the devil. His death and resurrection were literally the devil's undoing. Once captive to sin, we are now free through Christ's atoning work. "The law of the Spirit of life in Christ Jesus has made me free from the law of sin and death" (Ro. 8:2). Jesus has liberated us. "When he ascended on high he led a host of captives, and he gave gifts to men" (Eph. 4:8, ESV). As the King James Version puts it, "He led captivity captive."

Scottish theologian James Stewart wrote powerfully regarding this thrilling release: "It is a glorious phrase—'He led captivity captive.' The very triumphs of His foes, it means, He used for their defeat. He compelled their dark achievements to subserve His ends, not theirs. They nailed Him to a tree, not knowing that by that very act they were bringing the world to His feet. They gave Him a cross, not guessing that He would make it a throne. They flung Him outside the city gates to die, not knowing that in that very moment they were lifting up the gates of the universe, to let the king come in. They sought to root out His doctrines, not understanding that they were implanting imperishably in the hearts of men the very name they intended to destroy. They thought they had God with His back to the wall, pinned helpless and defeated: they did not know that it was God Himself who had tracked them down. He did not conquer in spite of the dark mystery of evil. He conquered through it."[10]

In his epic work *Cur Deus Homo?* (Latin for *Why did God become Man?*) eleventh century theologian, Anselm, sees Christ's death as the satisfying payment for our affront to God's holiness by our sin. He paid the penalty for our rebellion that God's perfect justice required. God's honor stays intact because the ground has been established whereby a perfectly holy God can forgive sinners. Christ's blood appeases God's wrath against sin and covers our sins by His mercy. Our English word for this stunning, unique display of love is propitiation. "In this is love, not that we loved God, but that He loved us and sent His Son to be the propitiation for our sins" (1 Jn. 4:10).

Building on Anselm's observations later Protestant reformers viewed Christ's sacrifice primarily through the lens of substitution. He took our place, receiving in Himself the punishment for sin we deserved. "For Christ also suffered for sins once for all, the righteous for the unrighteous, that He might bring you to God" (1 Pet. 3:18). This is why His sacrifice is often spoken of as a "vicarious" atonement.

Charles Spurgeon noted, "I have always considered with Luther and Calvin that the sum and substance of the gospel lies in that word substitution—Christ standing in the stead of man. If I understand the gospel, it is this: I deserve to be lost forever; the only reason why I should not be damned, is this, that Christ was punished in my stead, and there is no need to execute a sentence twice for sin."[11]

The atonement made through Jesus' sacrifice is so magnificent, so dazzling that it must be seen from many different vantage points. All of these viewpoints have merit, yet none of them alone can fully describe Jesus' amazing transaction that brought us back to God.

I'm appalled that some preachers think they have "graduated" beyond the gospel in their preaching. Such a notion only shows they have never taken a long, loving look at the atonement and the One who procured it. For if they really looked they would see that the gospel is forever fascinating and that all other subjects of any worth are subservient to this good news and orbit around it.

LOOK AND LIVE!

One of the most sublime confessions concerning Jesus Christ also serves as a summary statement of how the Scriptures reveal Him:

> We believe in one Lord, Jesus Christ, the only begotten Son of God, eternally begotten of His Father, God of God, Light of Light, Very God of Very God, begotten, not made, being of one substance with the Father, by whom all things were made: who for us and for our salvation came down from heaven, and was incarnate by the Holy Spirit of the virgin Mary, and was made man, and was crucified under Pontius Pilate. He suffered and was buried, and the third day He rose, according to the Scriptures, and ascended into heaven, and sits on the right hand of the Father. He shall come again with glory to judge the living and the dead, whose kingdom shall never end.
>
> —The Nicene Creed, 325 A.D.

It is to this all-sufficient Christ we are to look for every need.

Jesus doesn't need a makeover. We don't need to rebrand Him, we just need to unveil Him. For once He is seen for who He is, His power and glory forever impact us. Some are captivated by His love. Others are repelled by His claims. But once you really see Him you can never just walk away. Everyone who sees Him must deal with Him. He is too colossal to ignore.

> Jesus doesn't need a makeover. We don't need to rebrand Him, we just need to unveil Him.

When anyone truly encounters Jesus, there will indeed be some kind of response. Jesus' enemies were thrown to the ground by the sheer authority in His voice (Jn. 18:6). When Jesus exposed the hypocrisy of religious leaders they "sought to kill Him" (Jn. 5:16). A pagan Roman officer watched Him die and immediately changed his whole belief system (Mk. 15:39). Saul of Tarsus was thrown to the ground and blinded by His light (Ac. 22:7-11). John, Jesus' friend, saw Him in His splendor and "fell at His feet as dead" (Re. 1:17). But Jesus then called John to come nearer to Him and, unafraid, get a closer look at His majesty (Re. 1:17-18). This is the authority, glory, and eminence of the God-Man.

And so He calls you today. Look in wonder. Draw close in love. Look—and live (Nu. 21:9; Jn. 3:14-15).

Look to Jesus, your Savior. "God exalted this man to His right hand as ruler and Savior" (Ac. 5:31, HCSB). Through His blood He has saved us from sin's penalty and its power. Ultimately, we will be saved from sin's very presence as the gospel culminates in "new heavens and a new earth in which righteousness dwells" (2 Pet. 3:13). Anticipating His return and rule, we "eagerly wait for the Savior, the Lord Jesus Christ" (Phil. 3:20).

The late Rev. D. M. Stearns wrote a booklet titled *Message of the Cross* that was circulated in the millions. After preaching in Philadelphia a stranger came up to him and said, "I don't like the way you spoke about the cross. I think that instead of

> Jesus is the *greatest* example of splendid humanity, but He is the *only* candidate who ever qualified to carry the title, *Savior.*

emphasizing the death of Christ, it would be far better to preach Jesus, the teacher and example."

Stearns replied, "If I presented Christ in that way, would you be willing to follow Him?" "I certainly would," the stranger said. "All right then, let's take the first step. He did no sin. Can you claim that for yourself?" "Why, no. I acknowledge that I do sin." "Then your greatest need is to have a Savior, not an example."[12]

Jesus is the *greatest* example of splendid humanity, but He is the *only* candidate who ever qualified to carry the title, *Savior.* Look away from yourself, look away from your sin—and look to Him.

Look to Jesus, your redeemer. To redeem means to purchase or buy back. Jesus has purchased us at the highest possible price. Therefore, we are to be exclusively His. Christ "gave Himself for us that He might redeem us from every lawless deed and purify for Himself His own special people, zealous for good works" (Titus 2:14).

Look to Jesus, your substitute. He died the death we should have died, taking the punishment for sin we deserved. God "made Him who knew no sin to be sin for us, that we might become the righteousness of God in Him" (2 Cor. 5:21). This is truly the Great Exchange. Isaiah prophetically declared, "The Lord has laid on Him the iniquity of us all" (Isa. 53:6). The original Hebrew is much more graphic. A literal translation could read, "The Lord has smashed on Him the iniquity of us all." Don't ever think God's grace comes cheap.

Look to Jesus, your life-giver. "And you He made alive, who were dead in trespasses and sins" (Eph. 2:1). When we turn to Christ and trust His all-sufficient accomplishment for us everything changes. There is new life because there has been new birth. "Anyone who belongs to Christ has become a new person. The old life is gone; a new life has begun!" (2 Cor. 5:17, NLT). Before we came to Christ, the enemy of all life had a stranglehold on us, choking all hope. "The thief's purpose is to steal and kill and destroy," Jesus said. "My purpose is to give them a rich and satisfying life" (Jn. 10:10, NLT).

Look to Jesus, your friend and brother. Jesus displayed the zenith of love when He laid down His life for us as His friends (Jn. 15:13). But it gets even better than that—much better. Not only are we His friends, we're family! "Both the one who makes people holy and those who are made holy are of the same family. So Jesus is not ashamed to call them brothers and sisters" (Heb. 2:11, NIV). Astounding.

Look to Jesus, your lord. As a Christ-follower, you're under new management. We come to Christ, yielding our future to Him. "If you confess with your mouth Jesus as Lord, and believe in your heart that God raised Him from the dead, you will be saved" (Ro. 10:9, NASB).

In your joys, look to Jesus. In your sorrows look to Jesus. In life's blessings, look to Jesus. In life's pains—look to Jesus. Look and live! Jared Wilson urges us to wake up and look up:

> "Only the vision of Jesus makes sense of a broken world. He gives meaning to and fulfills suffering. He is the answer to the instinctual cry for justice. He is the ultimate threat to evil. He is the ultimate hope for deliverance. He is the puzzle piece that fits the eternity-shaped hole in the heart of man. . . . Jesus is big enough to fit into infinity. He is the true light of the world. He is the risen King, the exalted Lord. He is before all things and in him all things come together. All things were made through him and for him. That he might be preeminent to them and supreme over them. He is the radiance of God's glory.

51

One day we won't need the sun, because he will be the lamp of the new heavens and the new earth. Why in the world do we fix our eyes on anything but him?"[13]

FINISHED

After preaching some years ago in Bristol my host invited me to visit "Toplady's rock," not far away in the beautiful English countryside. The story is often told that Rev. Augustus Toplady took refuge from a sudden thunderstorm in the crevice of a large rock at Burrington Coomb in southern England. After the storm had passed, according to the story, Toplady was inspired to pen some of the most familiar words in English hymnody. Whatever the hymn's origins, potent theology is in every line:

Rock of Ages, cleft for me, let me hide myself in Thee;
Let the water and the blood from Thy riven side which flowed,
Be for sin the double cure, save from wrath and make me pure.

Toplady saw Christ's sacrifice as the "double cure" for our greatest needs before God—deliverance from His judgment of sin and deliverance from sin's power in our lives. Therefore, he appealed to Christ's sacrifice to "save from wrath and make me pure."

Not the labor of my hands can fulfill Thy law's demands;
Could my zeal no respite know, could my tears forever flow,
All for sin could not atone, Thou must save, and Thou alone.[14]

We acknowledge our abject inability to attain righteousness by our own merits and fulfill God's righteous demands. Christ and Christ alone can save us. That day as I wedged my body into the cleft of Toplady's rock, I was reminded vividly that believers in

Christ have a strong, safe refuge from judgment in the riven side of our Savior, the Rock of Ages who was "cleft for us."

The glory of the gospel is encapsulated in Christ's pronouncement from the cross, "It is finished!" (Jn. 19:30). This phrase is a single word in the original Greek language of the New Testament—*tetelestai*. It simply means paid in full. "This Man, after He had offered one sacrifice for sins forever, sat down at the right hand of God" (Heb. 10:12). Mission accomplished! This was not a cry of agony, it was a declaration of victory. God's justice had been satisfied.

Religions other than biblical Christianity start with *do* and *don't*. Our faith begins with *done!*

Theologian F. W. Krummacher noted, "He had now reached the final completion of His work of redemption. The exclamation, 'It is finished!' resounded in heaven and awoke hallelujahs to the Lamb which shall never more be mute. They reverberated through the abodes of darkness, like the thunders of God, announcing the termination of the dominion of their prince. But a more blissful sound on earth does not strike the ear of the penitent sinner to this hour than the words, 'It is finished!' It is the sound of the great jubilee trumpet, and the proclamation of an eternal salvation."[15]

Religions other than biblical Christianity start with *do* and *don't*. Our faith begins with *done!* All that was necessary to bring us back to God and make us righteous in His sight was accomplished completely and forever through Christ's sacrifice in our behalf. God's torrential judgment against sin was fully satisfied.

Above All

When I was a little boy I liked to play with a magnifying glass.

Holding this glass a few inches from my hand, I could see lines and creases not seen by the naked eye. Putting the magnifier close to the ground, small bugs could look like man-eating monsters. When magnified, things quickly got out of real-life proportion. It was somehow comforting to remove the magnifier and once again give true size to things.

But this doesn't work when we contemplate the greatness of God's almighty Son. For only by magnifying Him can we even begin to grasp His true "size"—the infinite expanse of His love, His holiness, and His glory.

In David's call to worship, he says, "Oh, magnify the Lord with me, and let us exalt His name together" (Psa. 34:3). To magnify means to make large or make larger. Of course, this doesn't mean we make God the Son larger than He already is. That would be impossible. His glory fills the universe. It means He is made larger in our perception of Him.

Some lenses are crafted to either magnify or reduce the true size of objects. Too often we tend to magnify our troubles while we reduce the size and scope of God Incarnate. The inverse should be the way we view life—the true proportion of our problems is smaller than what we perceive. And the "size" of Jesus Christ? He is the omnipotent God clothed in human flesh.

Are you magnifying your problems—while reducing God's true size? I have a word from the Word for you today: Magnify the Lord! There is nothing too hard for Him. "The reason some of us are such poor specimens of Christianity," wrote Oswald Chambers, "is because we have no almighty Christ."[16] Years ago J. B. Phillips wrote an important little book with the provocative title, *Your God Is Too Small*.[17] Is your God too small? Is your perception of Him too little and limited? Come now to the almighty Christ!

In *Prince Caspian* (C. S. Lewis's second book published in the *Chronicles of Narnia* series), young Lucy experiences a return visit from her majestic lion-friend, Aslan. Throughout the series

Aslan is portrayed as a type of Christ.

> Lucy: "Aslan, you're bigger."
> Aslan: "That is because you are older, little one."
> Lucy: "Not because you are?"
> Aslan: "I am not. But every year you grow, you will find me bigger."[18]

God does not grow, grow older, or get bigger. But, as "frail children of dust"[19] we grow—and we grow old. Hopefully, in our perception of things we also get bigger. How? By magnifying Him. We will never have to regret that we over-exalted King Jesus or magnified Him too much. Every year we grow in Christ, we find Him bigger.

Crucified and risen Christ now reigns over all. The Father is so pleased with His Son's atoning work that He has placed the coming judgment of the world under His jurisdiction. "He has set a day when He is going to judge the world in righteousness by the Man He has appointed. He has provided proof of this to everyone by raising Him from the dead" (Ac. 17:31). Now "God also has highly exalted Him and given Him the name which is above every name" (Phil. 2:9-10).

> *We look at this Son and see the God who cannot be seen. We look at this Son and see God's original purpose in everything created. For everything, absolutely everything, above and below, visible and invisible, rank after rank after rank of angels—everything got started in him and finds its purpose in him. He was there before any of it came into existence and holds it all together up to this moment. And when it comes to the church—he organizes and holds it together, like a head does a body.*
>
> *He was supreme in the beginning and—leading the resurrection parade—he is supreme in the end. From beginning to end he's there, towering far above everything, everyone. So spacious is he, so*

roomy, that everything of God finds its proper place in him without crowding. Not only that, but all the broken and dislocated pieces of the universe—people and things, animals and atoms—get properly fixed and fit together in vibrant harmonies, all because of his death, his blood that poured down from the cross (Col. 1:15-20, MSG).

It's hard, if not impossible, to read that and stay neutral. Either this gospel concerning Jesus is the most riveting, life-giving revelation ever delivered or it is history's most egregious lie. It's not surprising then that the laser of opposition today isn't so much against God in general, it's against Jesus in particular. Jesus Christ—His name, His gospel, His rule—has always been the point of contention. And not since the first century has the very mention of Him caused so much controversy. "Since September 11, 2001, I have seen more clearly than ever how essential it is to exult explicitly in the excellence of Christ crucified for sinners and risen from the dead," writes John Piper. "Christ must be explicit in all our God-talk. . . . God-in-Christ is the only true God and the only path of joy." [20]

No wonder those who oppose the gospel want to either bury the very mention of His name or only use it blasphemously. But Hebrews 1:1-3 invigorates our hearts and hopes, assuring us that *Jesus* has been appointed heir over everything. *Jesus* is "the brightness of [the Father's] glory and the express image of His person." *Jesus* at this present moment is "upholding all things by the word of His power."

In Christ

It was my privilege to meet Oswald J. Smith, the renowned missionary-statesman, shortly before he died. This Toronto pastor built one of the world's foremost missionary sending churches. He also wrote great songs that served as staples for many years in churches around the world. Perhaps his most popular song tells of the life-transforming impact of a real encounter with Jesus Christ:

> *When Jesus comes, the tempter's power is broken,*
> *When Jesus comes, the tears are wiped away.*
> *He takes the gloom and fills the life with glory,*
> *For all is changed when Jesus comes to stay.*[21]

Yes, the gospel changes everything. More specifically, Jesus, the vortex of the gospel, changes everything when we encounter Him and yield our lives to Him. Jesus Himself told us how we obtain eternal life when He prayed, "This is eternal life, that they may know You, the only true God, and Jesus Christ whom You have sent" (Jn. 17:3).

This almighty Christ who is the focus of everything and for whom everything exists now invites us to literally attach our lives to His. We are to draw our life from Him in the same way branches draw their life from the vine (Jn. 15:4-5).

The apostle Paul lumps all humanity into just two groups— those who are "in Adam," and those who are "in Christ." Tracing to our first parent, we inherit his fallen nature. We are sinners, not only because of what we've done; even more fundamentally we are sinners because of who we are. In this fallen state we are literally rebellious by nature. In two different letters, Paul describes all descendants of Adam as "sons of disobedience" (Eph. 2:2; 5:6; Col. 3:6). As such, we were destined for the coming judgment when God's holy wrath will be poured out against sin. This is the dreadful future of those who do not turn away from their sin. But in His love and kindness God has given a way to escape this future terror. He sent a substitute to incur this wrath in our place. And when we meet Jesus through repentance and faith we no longer tie our lineage to Adam, the rebel. Rather, we are now aligned with—and in the family of—Jesus, the redeemer! "He has delivered us from the power of darkness and conveyed us into the kingdom of the Son of His love" (Col. 1:13). As the old hymn writer put it, this is indeed "love divine, all loves excelling!"[22]

Once estranged from God and His blessings, we now have full access to Him and His care *in Christ* (Eph. 2:13). We are now His children through faith *in Christ* (Gal. 3:26). We are a new creation *in Christ* (2 Cor. 5:17). There is no condemnation because we are *in Christ* (Ro. 8:1). So there's no more need to hide. Just as fully as the Father accepts Jesus, the eternal Son of His love, He fully accepts us because we are *in Christ*. We are "accepted in the Beloved" (Eph. 1:6). No wonder A. J. Gordon exclaimed, "Nothing is more striking than the breadth of application which this principle of union with Christ has in the gospel. . . . it lifts all [believers] into a new sphere, and puts on them this seal and signature of the gospel, in Christ. So that while all things continue as they were from the beginning, all, by their readjustment to this divine character and person, become virtually new."[23]

One of the greatest hymns that shows the power of Christ's advocacy for us and our union with Him has only recently been rediscovered. It lay dormant in dusty English hymnals for over a century, almost never sung. A few years ago a new, memorable tune breathed new life into these potent lyrics. Now its truths are once again being sung in churches worldwide. If I were a theology professor, I might call these three power-packed stanzas Christology 101:

> *Before the throne of God above*
> *I have a strong and perfect plea,*
> *A great high priest whose name is Love*
> *Who ever lives and pleads for me.*
> *My name is graven on His hands,*
> *My name is written on His heart.*
> *I know that while in heaven He stands*
> *No tongue can bid me thence depart.*

When Satan tempts me to despair
And tells me of the guilt within,
Upward I look and see Him there
Who made an end of all my sin.
Because the sinless Savior died
My sinful soul is counted free.
For God the just is satisfied
To look on Him and pardon me.

Behold Him there, the risen Lamb,
My perfect spotless righteousness,
The great unchangeable I AM,
The king of glory and of grace.
One with Himself I cannot die,
My soul is purchased by His blood,
My life is hid with Christ on high,
With Christ my Savior and my God![24]

I've quoted a number of songs about Jesus in this chapter. I make no apology for that. He jumpstarts singing in every believing heart. I feel I'm on safe ground in asserting that no subject (even love itself) and certainly no other person has been the inspiration for more music than the person and saving work of the Lord Jesus Christ. This chapter could go on forever. I identify with John when he wrote, "There are also many other things that Jesus did, which if they were written one by one, I suppose that even the world itself could not contain the books that would be written" (Jn. 21:25). Such is the majesty of Jesus. In fact, throughout eternity God will just keep unpacking His love for us in Christ. "That in the ages to come He might show the exceeding riches of His kindness toward us in Christ Jesus" (Eph. 2:7).

What a message. What a Savior!

In our finiteness we could never know the triune God fully. But what dimensions of Him we do know we can know truly through the Scriptures and our daily walk with Him. As John Stott observed, "The riches of Christ are unsearchable. Like the earth, they are too vast to explore, like the sea too deep to fathom. They are untraceable, inexhaustible, illimitable, inscrutable and incalculable. What is certain about the wealth Christ has and gives is that we shall never come to an end of it."[26]

These riches are indeed endless. So let's peel back yet another layer of this "grace upon grace" and explore the strength and beauty that anchor us in the gospel.

THREE

THE GOSPEL—
COMPELLED BY ITS BEAUTY

But when the kindness and the love of God our Savior toward man appeared, not by works of righteousness which we have done, but according to His mercy He saved us, through the washing of regeneration and renewing of the Holy Spirit, whom He poured out on us abundantly through Jesus Christ our Savior.

Titus 3:4-6

The history of the world reduces to this: you being pursued by love.
Richard Swenson, M.D.
Margin

Romance is at the heart of the universe.

The gospel is a rescue story, a redemption story, a love story. Everything God is doing in history culminates in His fashioning a bride for His Son. Yet somehow the majesty and beauty of the gospel has been lost, even to most Christians. Someone has observed that much of modern evangelicalism reads like an IRS 1040 form: It's true, all the data is there, but it doesn't take your breath away.[1]

But a real look at the grandeur of the gospel will leave you breathless. As highlighted in the last chapter, Jesus—the subject of this Good News—is breathtaking. The prophet Haggai gives Him the beautiful title, "the Desire of all Nations" (Haggai 2:7). I'll always remember the week I watched this desire for Jesus on full display in the lives of thousands who had lived all their lives under communism's heavy hand.

Ever since I was called to preach as a teenager I had dreamed of an opportunity like this. A prayer of many young preachers in the Western world who had been called to ministry in the Cold War years was, "Lord, somehow, some way, someday let me preach the gospel behind the Iron Curtain."[2]

Communism's atheistic ideology had kept hundreds of millions essentially closed to Christian missions throughout my youth. But suddenly, as the 1990s dawned, God engineered epochal, turbulent change. The Berlin Wall came down. Joyful throngs filled the streets of Eastern Europe's cities as the elixir of freedom brought hope for the future. And the inconceivable happened. The Union of Soviet Socialist Republics vanished from the face of the earth.

In this dramatic twist of history, the ministry I could only dream of was then reality. There I was, standing in a side room in back of a stage in the Belorussian city of Minsk, ready to walk on stage and proclaim the beautiful gospel message.

But would anyone come to hear it?

I paced the floor of the little room and prayed, "Lord, we've stepped out in faith and rented this auditorium that seats 1200 people." (By the way, one of the few things the communists did right was build grand concert halls in almost every city. Little did they realize they were building them for evangelistic meetings!) "Why would anyone be interested in hearing some preacher from Texas? All we've done is rent this hall and distribute a few flyers about the meetings. Lord, please put at least a few hundred people in those seats."

Taking a deep breath I walked on stage. I was dumbfounded at what I saw. Huge crowds had showed up. And so had God. Not only was every seat taken, hundreds more were standing around the walls. Guards were posted at the entrance to the balcony. So many people had stuffed the balcony they feared it might collapse.

The response was even more thrilling. When I appealed to the people to respond to the gospel and commit their lives to Christ hundreds literally ran to the front, eager, even desperate, for new life in Jesus Christ. I especially recall the response of a burly Belorussian man with a huge moustache. After the service he came to me with tears in his eyes. He gave me a big bear hug and in broken English he exclaimed, "This is the most wonderful story I have ever heard!"

I assured my new brother in Christ that the gospel is the most wonderful story I have ever heard, as well. This gospel is the

> This gospel is the astounding announcement that all of God's pure wrath against sin landed on His Son. Now, with His righteousness fully intact, God can be both "just and the one who justifies those who have faith in Jesus." You won't find a story like *that* anywhere else!

astounding announcement that all of God's pure wrath against sin landed on His Son. Now, with His righteousness fully intact, God can be both "just and the one who justifies those who have faith in Jesus" (Ro. 3:26, NIV). At the cross "mercy and truth have met together; righteousness and peace have kissed" (Psa. 85:10). You won't find a story like *that* anywhere else!

Beauty for Ashes

Paul wrote, "Anyone who belongs to Christ has become a new person. The old life is gone; a new life has begun!" (2 Cor. 5:17, NLT). God Himself provided the supreme sacrifice for sin (Gen. 22:8). God the Son laid down His life for us. Paul actually says that God purchased our salvation "with His own blood" (Ac. 20:28). "It is crucial... to remember that the Christian faith has always understood that Jesus Christ is God," writes Timothy Keller. "God did not, then, inflict pain on someone else, but rather on the Cross absorbed the pain, violence, and evil of the world into himself. Therefore the God of the Bible is not like the primitive deities who demanded our blood for their wrath to be appeased. Rather, this is a God who becomes human and offers his own lifeblood in order to honor moral justice and merciful love so that someday he can destroy all evil without destroying us."[3]

Millions the world over can testify to the reality of the gospel's great exchange—beauty for ashes, joy for mourning, a life clothed in praise instead of heaviness (Isa. 61:3). William Tyndale, who would pay with his life for being the first person to print the Bible in English, wrote that the *euangelion* which we translate *gospel* is "a Greek word signifying good, merry, glad and joyful news, that makes a man's heart glad and makes him sing, dance, and leap for joy."[4]

When Phillip first took the gospel beyond Jerusalem and preached this good news throughout Samaria the result was "there was great joy in that city" (Ac. 8:8). Our world today is much like Samaria prior Phillip's evangelistic outreach. There's a critically short supply of hope, forgiveness, and joy. But the gospel gushes with all of the above and much more! Despair evaporates in hope. Forgiveness erases shame. Joy replaces sorrow! God's grace, what a message!

No wonder Timothy Keller writes, "If we are saved by grace

alone, this salvation is a constant source of amazed delight. Nothing is mundane or matter-of-fact about our lives. It is a miracle we are Christians, and the gospel, which creates bold humility, should give us a far deeper sense of humor and joy."[5]

Some might read this and think, "Tone it down a little. Don't get so emotional." But how can there not be an emotive, full-hearted response? It's an emotional subject—God gave His Son over to death for me! His Son took my sins on Himself. In exchange, He offers me pardon and His own family likeness. And it's all by grace through faith! Anyone who can muse on these things without some emotion surely needs a new birth. "Thanks be to God for His indescribable gift!" (2 Cor. 9:15).

At the Heart of the Universe

Doug Bannister observes, "Younger church members yearn to weave their life story within a larger script—a sacred romance in which God is both author and lover."[6] The Bible's integrating "larger script" is the awesome love story of how God Himself intervened to save His fallen creation, bent on self-destruction. God's eternal purpose is to call out a bride for His Son from fallen humanity. The composition of this beautiful, multi-ethnic bride will be redeemed people "out of every tribe and tongue and people and nation" (Rev. 5:9).

In the marriage union the bride typically assumes the surname of the groom. This is what happened as "God . . . visited the Gentiles to take out of them a people for His name" (Acts 15:14). We have assumed His name. We are *Christians*.[7] Our lives are now intertwined with His. As Paul Billheimer wrote, "A godly romance is at the heart of the universe and is the key to all existence. From all eternity God purposed that at some point in the future His Son should have an Eternal Companion, described by John the Revelator as 'the bride, the Lamb's wife.'"[8]

The Book of Ruth beautifully illustrates this aspect of Christ's redeeming love. Boaz voluntarily assumed his role as a kinsman-redeemer to the destitute widow, Ruth, and her mother-in-law, Naomi. In several ways throughout this short, poignant book Boaz pre-figures our kinsman-redeemer, Jesus Christ. By becoming a man while retaining His full deity and by willingly laying down His life for us, Jesus became both a kinsman and a redeemer to us. As our kinsman-redeemer, Jesus canopies our lives with His protective love and grace.

I saw just how far God will go to bring that grace to needy people in, of all places, a taxi cab in Manila, Philippines. As I sat in the back seat of that taxi cab in the Philippines, through the rearview mirror I could see that tears were in the driver's eyes. I was attending the Second Lausanne Congress on World Evangelization in Manila. Running a little late for a workshop at a hotel across the city, I had jumped into the first taxi I could wave down. Realizing that we had about a twenty minute ride, I took the opportunity to share the gospel with the cab driver.

As I told this man of God's love and Christ's sacrifice for him, I noticed that his eyes puddled with tears even more. That's when he asked if he could pull over and talk to me. Turning off the engine the cab driver faced me in the back seat and told me this amazing story.

"I don't know if you're going to believe this," he began, "but all night long I've been driving this taxi with a deep ache in my heart. This is the last hour of my shift. I've been driving through the streets of Manila crying out to God. In the last few days there's a phrase that keeps going over and over in my mind. Somewhere I heard someone talk about being *born again*. Through the night I've been longing to know what it really means," he continued. "I prayed, 'O God, it would be so wonderful to have a new start in life. I don't know what it means or how it happens. Please put someone in this cab who can tell me how I can be born again!'"

I marveled at the Father's tender mercies. God sent me all the way to the Philippines to bring living water to one thirsty cab driver. That's how much God loves people! What a joy it was to share the gospel and watch that man turn from his sins, pray to receive Christ, and then see his countenance literally change as he became a new creation in Christ. He experienced the new birth he had desperately sought!

It was so humbling to watch our sovereign God at work, engineering my schedule to intersect with one seeking heart. When I darted into the first available taxi I wasn't one cab too soon or one too late. God is very serious about getting the gospel to desperate people.

LOVE LANGUAGE

The sweet nectar of the gospel is encapsulated in four short yet poignant verses of Scripture:

- "Christ Jesus came into the world to save sinners" (1 Tim. 1:15). The gospel is the story of *the greatest rescue.*

- "He [God the Father] made Him who knew no sin to be sin for us, that we might become the righteousness of God in Him" (2 Cor. 5:21). The gospel is the story of *the greatest exchange.*

- "Believe on the Lord Jesus Christ and you will be saved" (Ac. 16:31). The gospel is the story of *the greatest assurance.*

- "For God so loved the world that He gave His only begotten Son, that whoever believes in Him should not perish but have everlasting life" (Jn. 3:16). The gospel is the story of *the greatest love.*

God's great love story assures us that all people, no matter their status, are of infinite worth. People are so valuable that heaven dispatched its greatest Prize to bring God's rebellious creation eternally home. John 3:16 is rightly termed "the heart of the Bible." Luther called it "the gospel in miniature."[9] I love the way John 3:16 begins in the Amplified Version: "For God so greatly loved and dearly prized the world that He [even] gave up His only begotten Son...." Here's a good way to unpack this good news:

God – the greatest lover
So loved – the greatest degree
The world – the greatest number
That He gave – the greatest act
His only begotten Son – the greatest gift
That whoever – the greatest opportunity
Believes – the greatest simplicity
In Him – the greatest attraction
Should not perish – the greatest promise
But – the greatest difference
Have – the greatest certainty
Everlasting life – the greatest possession[10]

"Greater love has no one than this," Jesus said, "than to lay down one's life for his friends" (Jn. 15:13). This is the love God showers on us from the cross. "We see clearly and receive fully God's love only in the cross of Christ," writes Larry Hart. "God's love is a *covenant* love. He calls us, in his gracious offer of salvation, into a *community* of love. He further joins us to his *kingdom* mission of spreading (and living) the message of his love."[11]

When Jesus saves us we get a new wardrobe! No longer are we clothed in the putrid rags of our own self-righteousness (Isa. 64:6). Now we are clothed in *His* righteousness (Ro. 13:14; Rev. 7:14). As renowned Bible teacher F. B. Meyer observed, "In His death He not only revealed the tender love of God but He put away our sins and wove for us those garments of stainless beauty in which we are gladly welcomed into the inner presence-chamber of the King."[12] Our sins are no longer exposed before His holiness. Instead, Jesus "covers our guilt with His obedience, and our deficiencies with His fullness."[13]

The gospel's love language laces the Scriptures.

This tender love language is our trump card in the brazen, often heartless world of the twenty-first century. While other religions and ideologies spew hate-filled bile, we declare the good news that all hostilities between God and man ceased at the cross! While some teach that the Almighty hates the infidel, the Bible assures us that while God has always hated sin He has always loved the sinner. And now that the sin barrier has been removed by Christ's sacrifice we can be declared righteous and once again connect with the God of perfect holiness. Jesus has now "reconciled all things to Himself... having made peace through the blood of His cross" (Eph. 3:20).

The gospel's love language laces the Scriptures. Further, God often employs visual aids to help us fathom the magnitude of this "so great a salvation" (Heb. 2:3). For instance, for those who know Jesus as Messiah every aspect of the Seder meal is rich with meaning and points to *Christ, our Passover* (1 Cor. 5:7). Just as a lamb is slain and becomes the central nourishment of this meal, so *Jesus Christ, the Lamb of God* was slain for us to bring wholeness and healing to all who partake of His life. This meal of remembrance harkens back to the terrible night when the Lord brought judgment on the people of the land. However, He provided a way for His people to be protected by their applying the blood of an innocent lamb to the doorposts of their dwellings. Then the Lord promised, "When I see the blood, I will pass over you; and the plague shall not be on you to destroy you" (Ex. 12:13).

Jesus directly compared His coming death to the scene when

Moses, following God's instructions, made a *bronze serpent* and lifted it on a pole in the midst of the people of Israel who were dying from venomous snakebites. This was God's judgment on their rebellion. When the people repented, God instructed Moses to lift up the bronze serpent for all to see. In response, "if a serpent had bitten anyone, when he looked on the bronze serpent, he lived" (Num. 21:9). Jesus said, "And as Moses lifted up the serpent in the wilderness, even so must the Son of Man be lifted up, that whoever believes in Him should not perish but have eternal life" (Jn. 3:14-15).

In the Scriptures serpents are a type of sin and rebellion. Sin's venom has infested all of humanity. Some Bible scholars see the reddish, copper color of the serpent on the pole suggesting the coming atonement Jesus would make with His blood. Now when we, in repentance and faith, look on Jesus who literally was made sin for us we too are healed from sin's poisonous effects (2 Cor. 5:21).

In the ancient world there were some compassionate men who purchased slaves—not to use or mistreat them but to free them. In the same way, *Christ our redeemer* purchases us out of the shame of the slave market, covers our nakedness, and frees us to a new life. This concept is so rich that two Greek words are employed in Scripture to help us understand the full scope of what it means to be redeemed. The Greek word *lutroo* denotes a very costly purchase. Our release came at the high price of the blood of God's Son. Jesus bought us, took us off the slave market, and has made us God's children and His very bride. Utterly amazing.

The second word, *agoridzo,* is a reference to the degradation and dehumanization of the slave market. When combined with the prefix *ex* (meaning out or out of) *exagoridzo* is a reference to "*a buyer* or *redeemer* who has gone to the slave market to purchase a slave for the solitary purpose of bringing him out of that place so he can be set free."[14] We were enslaved to sin. Sin was exacerbated by the requirements of the law. Our Redeemer came and purchased us with His blood. We have been permanently removed from captivity; we'll never be exposed for sale again!

It takes two words to appreciate the magnitude of our redemption. It also took two animals to help us comprehend how thoroughly Christ's sacrifice has dealt with our sins. We have seen typically how the first innocent animal was slain and its blood covered the people's sins. Under the Old Covenant this was only a temporary remedy. The ritual had to be repeated annually. But one day on a nondescript hill in Jerusalem God's perfect Lamb became the final, all-sufficient sacrifice for sin. "With his own blood—not the blood of goats and calves—he entered the Most Holy Place once for all time and secured our redemption forever" (Heb. 9:12, NLT). Jesus has mediated "a better covenant, which was established on better promises" (Heb. 8:6).

To augment our understanding of the amazing atonement Jesus would procure, a second *scapegoat* was brought before the priest under the Old Covenant. In this visual aid the high priest was instructed to "lay both his hands on the head of the live goat, confess over it all the iniquities of the children of Israel, and all their transgressions, concerning all their sins, putting them on the head of the goat, and shall send it away into the wilderness" (Lev. 16:21). This scapegoat was never seen again. It was gone, out of sight, and so were the people's sins that had been placed instead on it.

This symbolic transfer of the sins of the people onto the innocent animal prefigured how Jesus would take our sins on Himself and then take them away. Our sins, once placed on Him, are forever gone! "As far as the east is from the west, so far has He removed our transgressions from us" (Psa. 103:12). Talk about love language!

As mentioned earlier the *veil in the Temple* became perhaps the most dramatic visual aid of all. When Jesus cried out on the cross that the payment for sin had been fully paid, without warning the thick veil in the Temple was ripped from top to bottom. God Himself tore it open, granting access for everyone into His glory-filled presence.

This access to God is literally what anchors us in the gospel. It's what holds us steady in life's storms so that "we who have fled for refuge might have strong encouragement to seize the hope set before us. We have this hope as an anchor for our lives, safe and secure. It enters the inner sanctuary behind the curtain. Jesus has entered there on our behalf as a forerunner" (Heb. 6:18-20, HCSB). That's what we're confessing when we sing:

> *In every high and stormy gale,*
> *My anchor holds within the veil.*[15]

We're declaring that our place of refuge in all of life's turbulence is the presence of God. We have access to Him because Jesus broke through the barrier of sin that separated us from Him.

Finally, the rites Jesus ordained for His church are vivid illuminators of God's love for those who embrace the gospel. Both ordinances put the gospel on glorious display. In my opinion, although only followers of Jesus are to partake in these ordinances, unsaved family and friends should watch these ordinances being administered and their benefits received. Baptismal services and communion services can then become great evangelistic opportunities.

Through *baptism* the believer confesses his faith in a buried and risen Savior. This is the baptismal candidate's strong pronouncement that he or she is "all in" with Jesus. "We were buried with Him through baptism into death, that just as Christ was raised from the dead by the glory of the Father, even so we also should walk in newness of life" (Ro. 6:4).

At *the Lord's Supper* we symbolically partake of Christ's life and acknowledge the colossal price of redemption. By taking the broken bread we're declaring that Jesus' body was broken so we can be whole. By receiving the cup we remember that in order for new life to be poured into us Jesus' blood had to be poured out for us. This memorial is called "communion" for good reason. We enter into the power of the cross and commune with the Lord in a profoundly precious way as we identify with His transforming work. In fact, Paul actually says we are preaching the gospel each time we receive the elements. This becomes clear in the Greek verb used in 1 Corinthians 11:26: "For as often as you eat this bread and drink this cup, you *proclaim* the Lord's death till He comes" (italics added).

From whatever angle you survey the gospel all you see is grace and all you hear is the language of love. No wonder Spurgeon said, "Whitfield and Wesley might preach the gospel better than I do, but they could not preach a better gospel."[16]

GOSPEL GLORIES

Graeme Keith remembers that he was on an elevator with Billy Graham when another man in the elevator recognized the evangelist. He said, "You're Billy Graham, aren't you?" "Yes," Mr. Graham said. "Well," he said, "you are truly a great man." Mr. Graham immediately responded, "No, I'm not a great man, I just have a great message."[17]

A great message indeed. How well I remember being confronted by a college student already embittered by life. He blurted out through his tears, "I want you to prove to me that God loves me." I responded, "I'm so glad to tell you I can prove that. Just look at the cross. 'But God proves His own love for us in that while we were still sinners, Christ died for us!'" (Ro. 5:8, HCSB).

The gospel is not just about correct doctrine. It's about coming to know God personally through the mediating work of His Son. Prior to coming to Him in repentance and faith we were "without God and without hope in the world. But now in Christ Jesus you who once were far off are brought near by the blood of Christ" (Eph. 2:12-13). As John Piper observes, "Life is wasted if we do not grasp the glory of the cross, cherish it for the treasure that it is, and cleave to it as the highest price of every pleasure and the deepest comfort in every pain."[18]

The glories of the gospel are legion, as are the benefits that flow from it. Here are just a few. Through the gospel we have…

- *Salvation* for our lostness. "I am not ashamed of *the gospel* of Christ, for it is the power of God for salvation for everyone who believes" (Ro. 1:16).

- *Light* for our darkness. "…whose minds the god of this age has blinded, who do not believe, lest the light of *the gospel* of the glory of Christ, who is the image of God should shine on them" (2 Cor. 4:4).

- *Truth* for our confusion. "…the word of truth, *the gospel* of your salvation" (Eph. 1:13).

- *The Holy Spirit* for our seal. "…*the gospel* of your salvation, in whom also, having believed, you were sealed with the Holy Spirit of promise" (Col. 1:13).

- *Sonship* for our estrangement. "…that the Gentiles should be fellow heirs, of the same body, and partakers of His promise in Christ through *the gospel*" (Eph. 3:6).

- *Peace* for our fear. "…and having shod your feet with the preparation of *the gospel* of peace" (Eph. 6:15).

- *Hope* for our future. "…because of the hope which is laid up for you in heaven, of which you heard before in the word of the truth of *the gospel*" (Col. 1:15).

- *Life* for our death. "…our Savior Jesus Christ, who has brought life and immortality to light through *the gospel*" (2 Tim. 1:10).[19]

Throughout eternity God will just keep rolling out His kindness; "…that in the ages to come He might show the exceeding riches of His grace in His kindness toward us in Christ Jesus" (Eph. 2:7). This good news is not a message man would invent if he could. Nor is it a message he could invent if he would. As Ray Ortlund writes, "This gospel is a message to be believed and proclaimed (Mark 1:14-15). It is the point of the whole Bible (Gal. 3:8). It comes from God above (Gal. 1:11-12). It is worthy of our utmost (Phil. 1:27-30)."[20] It is well described as "…the glorious gospel of the blessed God which" Paul said, "was committed to my trust" (1 Tim. 1:11).

Now, in our time, you and I have received this sacred trust. God grant that the fragrance of this good news exude from our lives. Wherever we are, in every interaction, may we "come in the fullness of the blessing of the gospel of Christ" (Ro. 15:29).

Upon the gospel's sacred page
The gathered beams of ages shine;
And, as it hastens, every age
But makes its brightness more divine.

On mightier wing, in loftier flight,
From year to year does knowledge soar;
And, as it soars, the gospel light
Becomes effulgent more and more.

More glorious still, as centuries roll,
New regions blessed, new powers unfurled,
Expanding with the expanding soul,
Its radiance shall overflow the world.

Flow to restore, but not destroy,
As when the cloudless lamp of day
Pours out its floods of light and joy,
And sweeps the lingering mists away.[21]

How Beautiful

As a young man John Wesley had a deep reverence for God and was devout in daily reading from the Bible. As a student at Oxford he helped form "The Holy Club" and even went to the American colonies as a missionary. If salvation were obtained by good works young Wesley qualified. Yet Wesley himself was riddled with doubt, unsure of his standing before God. Without a personal assurance of salvation his attempts to minister to others were a total failure. One can sense the torture in his soul when he wrote, "I went to America to convert the Indians but, oh, who shall convert me? Who, what is He that will deliver me from this heart of mischief?"[22]

Back in England on May 24, 1738, he was sitting in a Bible study in a small chapel on Aldersgate Street in London. A Moravian was teaching from Martin Luther's preface to his commentary on Paul's Letter to the Romans. Wesley recorded in his journal: "About a quarter before nine, while [the speaker] was describing the change which God works in the heart through faith in Christ, I felt my heart strangely warmed. I felt I did trust in Christ, Christ alone, for salvation; and an assurance was given me that He had taken away my sins, even mine, and saved me from the law of sin and death."[23] His striving to be good enough to somehow merit salvation surrendered that night to a total embrace of the sufficiency of Christ. Soon after his conversion Wesley would translate Nikolas Zinzendorf's hymn as his own testimony:

Jesus, Thy blood and righteousness
My beauty are, my glorious dress;
Midst flaming worlds, in these arrayed,
With joy I shall lift up my head.[24]

We have a *beautiful Savior*. He is *beautiful*. I'm not referring to physical beauty because His visage was so marred by His sufferings for us He was hardly recognizable. "We hid, as it were, our faces from Him; He was despised and we did not esteem Him" (Isa. 53:3). What makes Him beautiful is that He makes everything else beautiful. "We are completely dependent upon God's revealed Word for a reset of our sense of beauty," notes Albert Mohler. "After the fall, we are too easily seduced by the merely pretty; we are bought off by the superficial and the gaudy. According to the Scripture, the cross is beautiful, but it is not pretty. It is most beautiful when it is seen in light of what the world considers most ugly. Therein is the beauty of the suffering servant from whom the world turned its face."[25]

He is *Savior*. Larry Hart notes, "*Savior* emerges in the New Testament as perhaps the comprehensive title for the person and work of Christ."[26] Jesus has saved us from sin's penalty. Right now He saves us from sin's power. One day we will be forever united with Him, saved from the very presence of sin. He has delivered us from sin's bondage to a free, fruitful life. We've traded the insecurities of alienation from God for peace with God. His life in us saves us from a small, selfish existence and integrates us into the purposes of God in our time. "If when we were enemies we were reconciled to God by the death of His Son, much more, being reconciled, we shall be saved by His life" (Ro. 5:10).

Beautiful Savior! Lord of all nations!
Son of God and Son of Man!
Glory and honor, praise, adoration,
Now and forevermore be Thine![27]

Hopefully, you'll see on every page of this book that we have a *beautiful gospel*. Although we engage in spiritual combat against spirit-realm forces aligned against the gospel, unlike many of the gospel's enemies we do not seek to repress freedom of speech. We endorse full freedom of discourse. All Christians have ever asked is that the gospel be given a place at the table in the unhindered exchange of ideas. We do not in some phobic way aim to suppress opposing voices.

But this grand good news just has this strong preponderance that often silences its detractors when it is freely proclaimed. This gospel of Jesus Christ towers in splendor over every other message. May this not be the very reason why some supposed intellectuals quickly become intolerant? Isn't this what lies behind the concerted campaigns to suppress the gospel and eradicate the very mention of Jesus' name? Opponents fear the dynamism of the gospel. Set against the lusterless backdrops of other ideologies the gospel bursts with light. Its hope-filled announcement dazzles with joy, power, and answers.

I've focused in this chapter on the gospel's beauty. We've reveled in God's great love for us that answers to our deep-seated need to be both fully known and fully loved. But as stated in the last chapter, it's crucial to recall that the gospel is not first about us. Foremost, it's about Him. The benefits of the gospel are not merely ours. God Himself benefits. "I, even I, am He who blots out your transgressions for My own sake" (Isa. 43:25).

Our need of the gospel is eternally important. God's glory through the gospel is all-important.

Our salvation is for His glory. As Ray Ortland observes, "God, through the perfect life, atoning death, and bodily resurrection of Jesus Christ, rescues all his people from the wrath of God into peace with God, with a promise of the full restoration of his created order forever— all to the praise of the glory of his grace."[28]

Our need of the gospel is eternally important. God's glory through the gospel is all-important.

Finally, as those made right with God by faith in Christ we have a *beautiful future*. For the follower of Jesus the future is always bright. The gospel is good news for Planet Earth, as well. "We, according to His promise, look for new heavens and a new earth in which righteousness dwells" (2 Pet. 3:13). One of the well-loved Christmas carols refers to this joyous future, with Jesus at the center of it all. Although this carol is typically sung to announce Christ's first coming to Earth, it is actually a hope-filled assurance of what awaits us when He comes again.

> *No more let sin and sorrow grow*
> *Nor thorns infest the ground.*
> *He comes to make His blessing known*
> *Far as the curse is found.*

> *He rules the world with truth and grace,*
> *And makes the nations prove*
> *The glories of His righteousness*
> *And wonders of His love.*[29]

The Tower of London is the safe treasury for the priceless Crown Jewels of England. The dazzling brilliance of these regal crowns is breathtaking. The Queen's coronation crown alone contains 2783 diamonds, 277 pearls, 18 sapphires, 11 emeralds, and five rubies.

Yet as awe-inspiring as these regal crowns are, they cannot be favorably compared to the immeasurable beauty and worth of heaven's treasures. These treasures are secured for us through the gospel when, as a bride commits her future to her husband, we commit our future to Jesus in faith and love. "Eye has not seen, nor ear heard, nor have entered into the heart of man the things which God has prepared for those who love Him" (1 Cor. 2:9).

This beautiful, powerful gospel enables us who believe to literally get the last laugh. We are empowered to rejoice in difficulties and stare down death itself. All because of Jesus. As Calvin Miller wrote, "We will one day stand on our graves and laugh a free man's laughter."[30]

FOUR

THE GOSPEL—
CONVINCED OF ITS POWER

For I am not ashamed of the gospel, because it is God's power for salvation to everyone who believes, first to the Jew and also to the Greek.

Romans 1:16, HCSB

I know that the gospel is the power of God – the great means that He employs for the regeneration of our ruined world.

David Livingstone

The gospel's power transforms people and nations.

Through repentance and faith in Christ's saving work we experience freedom, forgiveness, and a future. When a critical mass of people believe and obey the gospel nations experience large-scale transformation.

Some years back I was ministering at a large conference in Thailand. Naomi and I were thrilled to see thousands of people in attendance, most of them young people. What made this scene even more encouraging was knowing that most of these young believers were first generation Christians. Most of their parents were still idol worshipers. But the gospel had rescued

> When the gospel comes—when Jesus comes—everything changes. Life is made over. *We* are made over.

these young men and women.

Their worship was intense and beautiful. I was especially moved by one young girl's worship that was drenched in a heartfelt demeanor of gratitude. After the service I mentioned to her how I appreciated her beautiful expressions of thanksgiving to the Lord. With joy in her eyes she said, "Sir, may I tell you my story?"

"I was born in the red light district of Bankok," she told me. "I was placed in prostitution when I was a little girl. It was the only life I knew. One day a pastor came and put down money for me. But unlike all the others his intent was not to harm me."

With tears in her eyes she continued, "Sir, he bought me. He took me out of that horrible life. He fed me and educated me. He brought me into his family as one of his own daughters. Most of all," she beamed, "he brought the gospel to me."

Then through her tears she smiled and said, "I know what it means to be redeemed."

That is the gospel's transforming power. When the gospel comes—when Jesus comes—everything changes. Life is made over. *We* are made over. "If anyone is in Christ, he is a new creation; old things have passed away; behold, all things have become new" (2 Corinthians 5:17). We have not resolved to do better. We have not been improved upon. We have been made new, literally born again. We know what it means to be redeemed.

Having been rescued we're moved by a holy imperative to go back into the fray and rescue others. New-made, gospel-driven people have graced the world with thousands of hospitals, colleges, safe houses, schools, and feeding centers. The gospel has set in motion more good for humanity than all other forces combined. It has accomplished what armies and governments could not. The gospel doesn't just change conditions, it changes people. These changed people then become agents of change. Through the gospel people are changed, cultures are transformed, and God is exalted.

THE POWER OF THE GOSPEL

Paul said the gospel itself is the very power of God. He succinctly summarizes the gospel's awesome might in Colossians 1:12-13: "Giving thanks to the Father who has *qualified* us to be partakers of the inheritance of the saints in the light. He has *delivered* us from the power of darkness and *conveyed* us into the kingdom of the Son of His love" (italics added). God qualifies us as His people and therefore as rightful recipients of the benefits of His Kingdom. "His divine power has given us all things that pertain to life and godliness through the knowledge of Him." (2 Pet. 1:3-4). The gospel frees us from sin's vice and shifts us out of the kingdom of darkness into the kingdom of light. As Paul Washer states, "The immeasurable power of God manifests itself in the gospel. Nothing less than the gospel can bring a man to repentance and faith. Nothing less than the gospel can transform a man from sinner to saint. Nothing less than the gospel can bring many sons home to glory!"[1]

> *Work and do the law commands*
> *But gives us neither feet nor hands.*
> *Far better news the gospel brings—*
> *It bids us fly and gives us wings!*[2]

The gospel is disdained by the world partially because of its demands but also because of its immense power. The entrance of the gospel requires that popular ideologies surrender to the gospel's authority. Without the convicting work of God's Spirit the world's corridors of power aren't willing to concede their positions. This sets the stage for the cosmic war. Who will rule over Planet Earth? Every moment in ways large and small the kingdom of light and the kingdom of darkness are in conflict. "But where sin increased, grace increased all the more" (Ro. 5:20, NIV). Light wins.

A widely-circulated treatise declares, "We believe that the gospel is the good news of Jesus Christ—God's very wisdom. Utter folly to the world, even though it is the power of God to those who are being saved, this good news is Christological, centered on the cross and resurrection: the gospel is not proclaimed if Christ is not proclaimed, and the authentic Christ has not been proclaimed if his death and resurrection are not central."[3]

As Matt Chandler writes, "Only the unadjusted gospel is the empowered gospel."[4] If you don't have the cross and the empty tomb, you don't have the gospel. Christ's death and resurrection are indeed central in God's story, and ours. The *kerygma* is the preaching of the good news of Jesus Christ, giving emphasis to His saving act in His cross and resurrection. This mighty display of God's love, power, and wisdom is ground zero for every Christian believer. "To locate the center of history one must bypass all these vast empires and the glittering names associated with them and find his way to a tiny land called the navel of the earth, the geographical center of the world," wrote Paul Billheimer. "And in that tiny land is a tiny hill called Calvary, where two thousand years ago a Man named Jesus was lifted up to die. And this writer submits that that tiny hill in that tiny land is the center of all history, not only of this world, but of all the countless galaxies and island universes of outer space from eternity to eternity."[5]

We've looked in some detail at the power of Christ's crucifixion and resurrection. But let's also remember His present-tense, all-powerful ministry of intercession. His advocacy in our behalf secures our standing before an altogether holy God. This is one of the most potent benefits of embracing the gospel. Now that we are His, Jesus serves as our high priest, literally pleading our case against all of the accusations of the devil against us. The Amplified Version helps us understand something of the scope of the ministry Jesus is undertaking in our behalf this very moment: "He is able to save to the uttermost (completely, perfectly, finally, and for all time and eternity) those who come to God through Him, since He is always living to make petition to God and intercede with Him and intervene for them" (Heb. 7:25, AMP). The next time the enemy assaults you and tries to tell you what a weak Christian you are, remind him what a mighty advocate Jesus is. "I am writing these things so that you may not sin," John penned in his first letter. "But if anyone does sin, we have an advocate with the Father—Jesus Christ the Righteous One" (1 Jn. 2:1, HCSB).

God's treasure, this thrilling good news, is now entrusted to us. We're to faithfully share God's love and message with everyone everywhere. Our job, our stewardship, is to invite everyone to be "partakers of His promise in Christ through the gospel." As did Paul, we too can count on God's power-filled enablement as we minister life through the gospel, "of which I became a minister according to the gift of the grace of God given to me by the effective working of His power" (Eph. 3:6-8).

Because of the gospel we live under "a better covenant, which was established on better promises" (Heb. 8:6). The law, the Old Covenant, revealed our sinful condition but had no capability to change our status. "For what the law was powerless to do because it was weakened by the flesh, God did by sending his own Son in the likeness of sinful flesh to be a sin offering" (Ro. 8:3, NIV).

The law could not raise us to new life, in this life or the next. But through the gospel believers receive eternal life the moment they put their faith in Christ. This resurrection life is not only a future gift after we die that will be activated when we rise from our graves to meet Him. It is that, but it's more. We have this resurrection life now! And we anticipate the day when we will experience the same mighty power that thrust Jesus out of the tomb. "God both raised up the Lord and will also raise us up by His power" (1 Cor. 6:14). Jesus promised, "Because I live, you will live also" (Jn. 14:19). Our future with Him is greater than we can possibly imagine.

A few years ago on a rainy East Texas spring day after speaking to hundreds of young people I went to a small cemetery in Garden Valley, Texas. I was there to thank God for the lives of two men of God buried there—Keith Green and Leonard Ravenhill.

As I walked to Keith Green's grave, I recalled that wrenching day in the summer of 1982 when this trailblazing musician-prophet was suddenly whisked into heaven at age 29 in a plane crash just beyond the property of Green's Last Days Ministries. Compounding the grief felt by multitudes of young Christians, Keith and Melody Green's three year old son, Josiah, and their two year old daughter, Bethany, also died in the crash.

The gravestone marking where Keith, Josiah, and Bethany are buried bears the hope-filled reminder that they are *Gone To Be With Jesus.*" Inscribed on the stone is John 12:24: "Except a grain of wheat falls into the ground and dies, it remains alone; but if it dies, it brings forth much fruit."

Keith's life and ministry continue to bear much fruit today as his passionate love for Jesus, so powerfully expressed through his timeless music, is rediscovered by a new generation. There at his grave I softly sang the song he and Melody had written shortly before his death:

> *There is a Redeemer, Jesus, God's own Son*
> *Precious Lamb of God, Messiah, holy One.*
>
> *Jesus, my Redeemer, Name above all names*
> *Precious Lamb of God, Messiah, O for sinners slain.*

When I stand in Glory, I will see His face
There I'll serve my King forever, in that holy place.

Thank You, O my Father, for giving us Your Son,
And leaving Your Spirit 'til the work on earth is done.[6]

POWER IN THE BLOOD

When I was a small boy at camp I remember singing,

There is power, power, wonder-working power
In the precious blood of the Lamb.[7]

John Newton, the clergyman who wrote *Amazing Grace*, knew this wonder-working power. A former slave ship master, after his conversion to Christ he rose to lead one of London's most influential churches. Yet remembering his former defiance against God Newton would often refer to himself as "the old African blasphemer."[8] Though ever-mindful of his pre-Christ wretchedness, he became one of England's best-loved gospel preachers and a strong advocate for ending the slave trade throughout the British Empire. On his deathbed he whispered to a friend, "My memory is almost gone. But I remember two things: that I am a great sinner and Christ is a great Savior."[9]

When we get to heaven, where all of the theological fog will have cleared, we will see clearly what (and who) got us there. No one in heaven will be extolling his own merits. On the contrary, our new song will be, "You were slain, and have redeemed us *by Your blood* out of every tribe and tongue and people and nation" (Rev. 5:9, italics added). What will be the focus of our praise in heaven? Jesus and His blood. What should be the focus of our praise here on Earth? Jesus and His blood.

Jesus' blood makes possible a new birth for us personally but also for the earth itself. As Matt Chandler explains, "The explicit gospel… magnifies God's glory as it heralds the supremacy of his Son… We see that the peace that is made by the blood of the cross covers 'all things.' The scope of Christ's reconciling work on the cross spans the brokenness between man and God *and* the brokenness between earth and heaven."[10]

It truly takes the entire New Testament to unpack the efficacy of Christ's blood spilled for us. For instance (and this is just a sampling), through the blood of Christ we have—

- *Propitiation.* "God presented Him as a propitiation through faith *in His blood*" (Ro. 3:25).

- *Justification.* "Much more then, since we have now been declared righteous *by His blood*, we shall be saved through Him from wrath" (Ro. 5:9).

- *Redemption.* "We have redemption in Him *through His blood*, the forgiveness of our trespasses, according to the riches of His grace" (Eph.1:7).

- *Fellowship.* "But now in Christ Jesus, you who were far away have been brought near *by the blood* of the Messiah" (Eph. 2:13).

- *Peace.* "And through Him to reconcile everything to Himself by making peace *through the blood* of His cross—whether things on earth or things in heaven (Col. 1:20).

- *Boldness.* "We have boldness to enter the sanctuary *through the blood* of Jesus, by a new and living way He has opened for us through the curtain (that is, His flesh)" (Heb. 10:19).

- *Sanctification.* "Jesus also suffered outside the gate, so that He might sanctify the people *by His own blood*" (Heb. 13:12).

- *Cleansing.* "But if we walk in the light as He Himself is in the light, we have fellowship with one another, and *the blood* of Jesus His Son cleanses us from all sin" (1 Jn. 1:7).

- *Victory.* "They conquered him *by the blood* of the Lamb and the word of their testimony, for they did not love their lives in the face of death" (Rev. 12:11).[11]

The blood of Christ is at work for you, right now. His blood keeps on cleansing us as we walk in the light of Christ's lordship. The blood of Jesus saved us from sin's penalty when we embraced the gospel. His blood is active at this moment, saving us from sin's power. The tense of the verb *cleanses* denotes a present, continuous activity.

> *It soothes my doubts and calms my fears,*
> *And it dries all my tears;*
> *The blood that gives me strength from day to day,*
> *It will never lose its power.*[12]

Some groups, in keeping with current sentiments and sensitivities, are systematically removing references to the blood of Jesus from their hymnals and readings. In doing this they are ripping out the very life of the gospel message. "The life of the flesh is in the blood" (Lev. 17:11). The life of Christian theology is in the blood, as well. "Without the shedding of blood there is no forgiveness of sins" (Heb. 9:22, ESV). Churches that have a so-called "gospel" minus the blood in fact just have a spiel minus the gospel. And any church that has forfeited the gospel has also forfeited its biblical right to exist.

Christians of an earlier era talked about "pleading the blood."

Churches that have a so-called "gospel" minus the blood in fact just have a spiel minus the gospel.

By this they meant that, knowing their authority in Christ, they could aggressively superimpose the efficacy of the blood of Jesus over and against any design of the devil leveled toward themselves or others. The power of the blood rendered all curses and evil intents null and void. God give us in our day faith-filled believers who know the blood's "wonder-working power" and who will "plead the blood" against all the schemes of the enemy.

Not only are we protected from the devil by Jesus' blood. We are also protected against God's wrath when He judges sin. We are protected from God's judgment in the same way the children of Israel were protected on that first Passover night when the Lord brought judgment on the people of the land. God provided a way for His people to be protected by applying the blood of an innocent lamb to the doorposts of their dwellings. Then the Lord promised, "When I see the blood, I will pass over you; and the plague shall not be on you to destroy you" (Ex. 12:13). The blood applied to the top of the door and on each side reminds us in a very pronounced way that we are protected under the New Covenant by our Lord's wounds on the cross.

The analogy here is so awesome we must pause and learn from that epochal night. Think of what any Hebrew mother must have experienced that night. Earlier that day along with her husband she had applied the blood of the innocent lamb to the doorposts of their dwelling. Then by faith they received the promise that God's judgment would pass over them because they were now protected by the blood and marked as those in covenant with Him.

But as Hebrew mothers held their firstborn sons that night they started to hear agonized shrieks from Egyptian mothers as death hit every home without the blood. Nationwide, Egyptian firstborn boys were inexplicably dying. Now, if you were in the place of those Hebrew mothers how would you have reacted?

I'm sure there were strong, spiritual women who remained perfectly calm. But let's get real. No doubt there were other Hebrew mothers who were frozen with fear as the wails of grief grew louder by the minute.

But here's the point—and it's a big one. Those frightened Hebrew mothers and their sons were *just as safe* as the saintly, serene mothers and their sons that night. Why? Because their safety did not rest in the level of their faith. Their safety was in the power of the blood!

In the same way our protection from God's wrath does not rest in what we have done but what He has done. Even if our faith may seem weak we "apply the blood" to our lives, where we live, and we too experience God's miracle of grace. Our salvation does not rest in the level of our faith but in the sufficiency of His sacrifice.

> *"This, the power of the cross:*
> *Christ became sin for us;*
> *Took the blame, bore the wrath—*
> *We stand forgiven at the cross.*
>
> *"This, the power of the cross:*
> *Son of God—slain for us.*
> *What a love! What a cost!*
> *We stand forgiven at the cross.*[13]

THE POWER OF A GOSPEL CULTURE

Both Jesus and Paul used the concept of leaven to illustrate how a smaller culture can influence and eventually permeate and fundamentally change another culture. Jesus warned against the spread of corrupting leaven. "Beware of the leaven of the Pharisees and the leaven of Herod," Jesus cautioned (Mk. 8:15). This was a caveat to all of Christ's followers not be altered at the core of our makeup by either hypocritical religion or corrupt government. Twice Paul reminded us, "A little leaven leavens the whole lump" (1 Cor. 5:6; Gal. 5:9).

But this truth is not just a warning. It's also a hope. There is also good, desirable leaven. Jesus said, "The Kingdom of heaven is like the yeast a woman used in making bread. Even though she put only a little yeast in three measures of flour, it permeated every part of the dough" (Matt. 13:33, NLT). The principle is that what begins in a small but potent measure can have untold ramifications, changing the very properties of a culture. The impact of Jesus on the world, which began in a backlot barn in an unimpressive town, will one day blanket the whole planet. "Of the increase of His government and peace there will be no end" (Isa. 9:7). Like good leaven, a gospel culture has invaded the mix of history. Its spread is already very substantial. One day this gospel will permeate and forever change the entire world. This will culminate in the full expression of God's kingdom.

The properties that comprise a culture are those elements we value greatly. Today we call them core values. We rejoice in these deep-seated convictions. However, these core values also represent what we will suffer for and if need be die for. The apostle Paul tied suffering for the gospel with experiencing God's power. This should encourage Christians worldwide as reprisals against gospel proclamation intensify. "Therefore do not be ashamed of the testimony about our Lord, nor of me his prisoner," Paul wrote, "but share in suffering for the gospel by the power of God" (2 Tim. 1:8, ESV). Here's the point Paul was making: If you want to experience God's power operating in your life, embrace the sufferings associated with being a gospel carrier.

The two letters of the apostle Peter are fairly short, but within these letters Peter vouchsafes those values he holds most dear, the elements he used like good leaven to form a gospel culture. But before we can fully understand Peter's core values (and make them our own) we need to see how our perception of an often-used word has changed over the years. That word is *precious*. Language tends to morph over time. In today's usage, "precious" has become feminized and is almost synonymous for "cute" or "sweet." But when Peter refers to something as precious he means it is rare, of surpassing value, and something (or someone) to be honored as beyond price. When Peter categorizes something as precious, he is giving us his list of non-negotiables, those things he places in highest regard—his core values.

First among these, Peter valued *the gospel of Christ*. Peter said a tested, authentic faith in Christ is "more precious than gold" (1 Pet.1:7). In his second letter he references other believers as those who possess "like precious faith" (2 Pet. 1:1). Peter was passionate about his faith in Christ. He cherished it as more precious than gold. He was willing to lay down his life for this precious faith. In fact, he did die as a martyr for the gospel. Is the gospel precious—priceless—to us? If so, we'll be willing to suffer for it. We will anchor our lives in it.

Flowing (literally) from his prizing of the gospel, Peter also valued *the blood of Christ*. He reminded his readers that they were purchased by "the precious blood of Christ" (1 Pet. 1:19). The message of redemption solely through the shed blood of Christ is under acerbic attack today in our pluralistic culture. Do we "cherish the old rugged cross"? Are we willing to suffer, even die, for it?

Third, Peter valued *the person of Jesus Christ*. The rarer the jewel, the greater the value. Christ is the one and only redeemer. He is "chosen by God and precious" (1 Pet. 2:4). Jesus is the "precious cornerstone" (1 Pet. 2:6). In grand understatement Peter writes, "To you who believe, He is precious" (1 Pet. 2:7). He is peerless, matchless, priceless.

Finally, Peter valued *the promises of Christ*. He called them "exceedingly great and precious promises" (2 Pet. 1:4). These awesome, trustworthy promises are our "tickets to participation in the life of God" (2 Pet. 1:4, MSG). These promises are grounded in the gospel. They empower us to escape the corruption in the world.

In an old advertising campaign of a major credit card company they listed some valuable things that could be bought using their card. But then the advertisement reminded us that, beyond the cost of what can be bought, some realities are simply priceless.

What is priceless to you? After God had deluged Abram with astounding wealth and assets He pulled him aside. In essence, God reminded Abram, "These are gifts from My hand but they have a shelf life. They're valuable, but they're not priceless. Abram, *I* am your reward" (See Gen. 15:1).

The good news we announce is that we humans, the inhabitants of a small planet in God's vast creation, can approach God unafraid, commune with Him, and even call Him "Father." This is the priceless, astounding power of the gospel. And these are the precious values that help constitute a gospel culture. Let's embrace Peter's core values. They all orbit around the gospel. Here is our sure bedrock. Here is where we drop anchor.

A gospel culture blooms in soil that is enriched both by sound doctrine and God's love. There is an ever-growing love relationship between the believer and the triune God. "We love Him because He first loved us" (1 Jn. 4:19). This love then spills over to all people in acts of generosity and kindness. "As we have opportunity let us do good to all," Paul wrote, "especially to those who are of the household of faith" (Gal. 6:10). While the world may not share our values they desperately want to see our gospel culture work. They want the church to act like the church. It is both to their benefit and ours.

Ray Ortlund addresses this clearly: "The test of a gospel-centered church is its doctrine on paper *plus* its culture in practice… If a church's gospel culture has been lost, or was never built, the only remedy is found at the feet of Christ. That church needs a fresh rediscovery of his gospel in all its beauty. It needs to prayerfully reconsider everything it believes and practices. Nothing is gained by merely repackaging the church in forms more attractive to outsiders… Any church in any denomination today that falls short of the gospel of Christ in either doctrine or culture will inevitably collapse under the extreme pressure of our times."[14]

To that I echo a hearty amen. The gospel's power is best seen when the love of God is best seen. We are to use God's power to display God's love. That brings us to the interplay of the Holy Spirit with the message of the gospel.

THE SPIRIT AND THE GOSPEL

Missiologist Gary Tyra writes, "The Holy Spirit is all about the enablement of Christ's followers to glorify the Father, in the name of the Son, in such a way as to encourage lost and hurting human beings to accept the invitation to join the divine dance, experiencing justification, sanctification and empowerment for ministry themselves in the process."[15] That is why some writers refer to the Holy Spirit as "the go-between God." The power in the gospel is the Spirit's work in applying the work of Christ to us personally.

God's Spirit is ever pointing people to Jesus. His primary job is to put the spotlight on Christ and His gospel. Jesus said, "But when the Helper comes, whom I shall send to you from the Father, the Spirit of truth who proceeds from the Father, He will testify of Me" (Jn. 15:26).

When we believed the gospel "he saved us, not because of the righteous things we had done, but because of his mercy. He washed away our sins, giving us a new birth and new life by the Holy Spirit" (Titus 3:5, NLT). The Spirit of God takes the message of God and drives it deep into hearts.

When we come in saving faith to Christ, the Spirit of God takes up residence inside us and begins to reconstruct us. God's Spirit within us "is able to do exceedingly abundantly above all that we ask or think, according to the power that works in us" (Eph. 3:20). The apostle Paul prayed that believers might know "what is the exceeding greatness of His power toward us who believe, according to the working of His mighty power which He worked in Christ when He raised Him from the dead" (Eph. 1:19-20). The same mega-power that raised Jesus from the dead is now working in us to raise us to the destiny for which we were born—and born again.

The Holy Spirit is all over the proclaiming of the gospel and the applying of its benefits. It is the Holy Spirit who—

- *Convinces us of our need of a Savior.* "And when He has come, He will convict the world of sin, and of righteousness, and of judgment" (Jn. 16:8).

- *Anoints the preaching of the gospel.* "For our gospel did not come to you in word only, but in power, and in the Holy Spirit, and in much assurance, as you know what kind of men we were among you for your sake" (1 Thess. 1:5).

- *Makes us new through the gospel.* "Not by works of righteousness which we have done but according to His mercy He saved us, through the washing of regeneration and renewing of the Holy Spirit" (Titus 3:5).
- *Seals and protects our standing with God.* "In Him you also trusted, after you heard the word of truth, the gospel of your salvation; in whom also, having believed, you were sealed with the Holy Spirit of promise" (Eph. 1:13).

- *Pours God's love into us and through us.* "The love of God has been poured out in our hearts by the Holy Spirit who was given to us" (Ro. 5:5).

- *Empowers us as witnesses for Christ.* "But you shall receive power when the Holy Spirit has come upon you; and you shall be witnesses to Me in Jerusalem, and in all Judea and Samaria, and to the ends of the earth" (Ac. 1:8).

- *Produces Christ-like fruit in our lives.* "But the fruit of the Spirit is love, joy, peace, longsuffering, kindness, goodness, faithfulness, gentleness, self-control" (Gal. 5:22-23).

- *Gifts us for effective service.* "There are diversities of gifts… But one and the same Spirit works all these things, distributing to each one individually as He wills" (1 Cor. 12:4, 11).

- *Moves us toward maturity in Christ.* "For as many as are led by the Spirit of God, these are the sons of God" (Ro. 8:14).

Why is such immense power readily made available to gospel believers? For us to launch a global movement, not of terror but, on the contrary, of compassion. Our weapons are entirely different from those employed by other armies and militias. And no effective counter has yet been found to our weapons! Bombs can be countered with bombs. Angry rhetoric can be countered with more of the same. Hate can be countered with hate. But aggressive love—how do you counter that? In our arsenal of power we have the power of the Spirit Himself, who then activates the power inherent in the gospel, God's Word, the name of Jesus, the blood of Jesus, and the love of Jesus.

This is the reason that the Spirit empowers us. He desires that we become, as T. L. Osborn said, "a mighty army whose soldiers of love are to reach every land and plant Christ's banner of salvation in every nation! As ambassadors of the King of kings, the Christian's business is to evangelize every land and 'take out of them a people for His name' (Acts. 15:14). This is the purpose of Pentecost."[16]

Frankly, I believe all Christians who are truly Spirit-filled are pre-set toward evangelism and missions. When the Holy Spirit descended on the Day of Pentecost Peter's powerful evangelistic message resulted in thousands of converts. When believers prayed for boldness in Acts 4, God answered by filling them with the Holy Spirit so that they boldly proclaimed the good news. Robert Coleman notes, "People full of the Holy Spirit are committed to God's work. They want to be where laborers are needed most, and there is no more pressing need than bringing the gospel to hell-bound men and women."[17]

As resistance to the gospel mounts there is an increased need for what many refer to as power encounters. In Jesus' ministry and in the ministries of the early Christian disciples, some kind of power encounter often verified their Spirit-anointed announcement of the good news. What is a "power encounter"? It is a visible demonstration that Jesus can overrule anything or anyone who tries to defy Him. John Wimber noted, "Any system or force that must be overcome for the gospel to be believed is cause for a power encounter."[18]

At a time of acute discouragement, John the Baptist requested reassurance that Jesus was indeed the Messiah. Jesus responded, "Go and tell John the things which you hear and see: The blind receive their sight and the lame walk; the lepers are cleansed and the deaf hear; the dead are raised up and the poor have the gospel preached to them" (Matt. 11:4-5). Jesus saw these miracles, or power encounters, as the verifying credentials of His ministry.

The only New Testament model we have for the ministry of the evangelist is Philip. The report of Philip's evangelistic event in Samaria is also a model for effective evangelism today.

"Then Philip went down to the city of Samaria and preached Christ to them. And the multitudes with one accord heeded the things spoken by Philip, hearing and seeing the miracles which he did. For unclean spirits, crying with a loud voice, came out of many who were possessed; and many who were paralyzed and lame were healed. And there was great joy in that city" (Acts 8:5-8).

Notice that Philip's audience did not just hear; they *heard and saw*. Philip's evangelistic ministry was first and foremost preaching the gospel of Jesus Christ. However, his preaching was augmented by a deliverance ministry and the working of miracles. The Scripture suggests that the people were not convinced of the veracity of Philip's message by his preaching alone. They "heeded the things spoken by Philip, hearing and seeing the miracles which he did."

Paul said he brought the nations to obey the gospel "in word and deed... in mighty signs and wonders, by the power of the Spirit of God" (Ro. 15:18-19). Using this three-fold strategy of gospel proclamation, compassionate works done in Jesus' name, and miracles, Paul said, "I have fulfilled the ministry of the gospel of Christ" (Ro. 15:19, ESV). Deeds of compassion generated by the gospel, along with miracles performed by the living Christ, help authenticate the gospel of Christ, demonstrate the reality of the kingdom of Christ, and remove barriers to the reception of Christ.

The Gospel of Mark concludes by saying that the ascended Christ continued to empower His disciples as they shared the gospel, "validating the Message with indisputable evidence" (Mk. 16:20, MSG).[19] Quoting T. L. Osborn again, "Whether it is Peter in traditional Jerusalem, Philip in immoral Samaria, or Paul on the pagan island of Melita, the same results always followed; they proclaimed the gospel, miracles were in evidence, and multitudes believed and were added to the church."[20]

Too often today we have softened the gospel's demands and

When the gospel is preached we need to expect Jesus to show up in power.

replaced its glory with lesser agendas. The church in the West is frequently guilty of trading in a robust gospel for an anemic facade. We've capped the wells of living water with unbelief. Let's get back to the gospel of Jesus Christ! When the gospel is preached we need to expect Jesus to show up in power. But when He shows up things can get uncomfortable, especially for those who "have a form of godliness but deny its power" (2 Tim. 3:4). As believers in Jesus, let's open the tap and believe that living water can gush from us to thirsty seekers (Jn. 7:38). We have plenty of biblical and historical precedent for expecting just that.

May God raise up mighty gospel proclaimers for this hour! And may you be one of them. We are in need of preachers who will "preach the gospel to you by the Holy Spirit sent down from heaven" (1 Pet. 1:12). We need marketplace missionaries who will bring the glory of Jesus into businesses and turn them into bases for evangelism and discipleship. We need hybrid healing evangelists who are also brilliant apologists. We need anointed media evangelists who have Holy Spirit savvy to leverage social media to give the gospel the largest possible audience and impact. We need steady, Spirit-filled witnesses for Christ in every arena of human interaction who will be salt and light in this decaying, dark culture.

The mighty work of the Spirit will keep changing us until we ultimately are conformed into the very image of Christ. "But we all, with unveiled face, beholding as in a mirror the glory of the Lord, are being transformed into the same image from glory to glory, just as by the Spirit of the Lord" (2 Cor. 3:18). Jerry Bridges notes, "As we behold the glory of the Lord as reflected in the gospel, the Holy Spirit uses the gospel as one of His transforming instruments."[21] No other message has such astounding power.

And no other message has spawned such an outpouring of love and passionate devotion.

> *Love so amazing, so divine,*
> *Demands my soul, my life, my all.*[22]

So let's focus now on the high standard that is the only worthy response to such amazing love.

FIVE

THE GOSPEL—
CALLED TO ITS STANDARD

Whatever happens, conduct yourselves in a manner worthy of the gospel of Christ.

Philippians 1:27, NIV

There are two things that they have need to possess who go on pilgrimage: courage and an unspotted life. If they have not courage, they can never hold on their way; and if their lives be loose, they will make the very name of the pilgrim stink.

John Bunyan
The Pilgrim's Progress

Our lives should attract people to the gospel, not repel them from it.

For us to be attractors we must let the gospel thoroughly change us. This begins by coming to Jesus on His terms. He calls us to fully embrace Him, His life, and His standard. Jesus has always called for a choice, a change: "Repent and believe in the gospel" (Mk. 1:15). This was not a multiple answer invitation. His hearers were confronted with a singular call for which there were only two responses, *yes* or *no*.

Our God is not a God of half measures. Yet in very early American history a regrettable precedent was set whereby those who gave just a nod to Christianity were afforded many of the privileges of the fully devoted. These "half-way covenanters," as they were called, claimed no personal conversion to Christ yet they and their children were still viewed as part of the church.[1] Their affiliation was something of a "family plan" for the quasi-committed.

Of course, this set the stage for an onslaught of compromise and theological liberalism. There are continuing ramifications from these centuries-old concessions that are still evident in American church life today. The potency of the gospel was diluted because of these accommodations to nominalism. We are always in danger if we seek to lessen the gospel's demands or lower its standards. Jesus said, "I have come as a light into the world, that whoever believes in Me should not remain in darkness" (Jn. 12:46, MEV).

We do not receive Christ in bits and pieces. Only those who live under His lordship truly honor His grace. Deitrich Bonhoeffer went so far as to assert, "The only man who has the right to say that he is justified by grace alone is the man who has left all to follow Christ."[2] We have been purchased by His blood. We belong to Him. We are to be exclusively His. "He died for all, that those who live should no longer live for themselves, but for Him who died for them and rose again" (2 Cor. 5:15).

There is a sense in which no one should feel qualified (in his own adequacy) to represent God's message of salvation. At the same time we should acknowledge that He has indeed qualified us and entrusted us with the gospel message. "Not that we are competent in ourselves to claim anything for ourselves, but our competence comes from God. He has made us competent as ministers of a

> To live in a manner worthy of the gospel means we embrace Christ's lordship, express His love, and boldly share His message.

new covenant" (2 Cor. 3:5-6).

To live in a manner worthy of the gospel means we embrace Christ's lordship, express His love, and boldly share His message. To accomplish this we draw on His life-giving Spirit and we live in light of eternity, remembering that we will give an account of our post-conversion lives when we stand before Jesus. In short, as Christians we are to live by the Spirit's power for the glory of God, the honor of Jesus, and the spread of the gospel.

THE STANDARD OF OBEDIENCE

Where did we get the idea that the lordship of Jesus Christ is an "available option" for those who call themselves Christians? This is the invention of some persuasive teachers but no such doctrine is found in the New Testament. In Jim Elliot's personal journals written when he was only twenty-two he called such a notion a "twentieth century heresy." This incisive young sage who would lay down his life for the gospel's advance just a few years later insisted that the gospel "must be preached with the full apprehension of who He is, the demanding Lord as well as the delivering Savior."[3]

Fortunately, the doctrinal statements of almost all evangelical churches are clear on this. Let's look at two representative statements of faith from two of the largest evangelical denominations. Note that in both statements "repentance toward God and faith toward our Lord Jesus Christ" are non-negotiables.

The Baptist Faith and Message states clearly, "Regeneration, or the new birth, is a work of God's grace whereby believers become new creations in Christ Jesus. It is a change of heart wrought by the Holy Spirit through conviction of sin, to which the sinner responds in repentance toward God and faith in the Lord Jesus Christ. Repentance and faith are inseparable experiences of grace. Repentance is a genuine turning from sin toward God.

Faith is the acceptance of Jesus Christ and commitment of the entire personality to Him as Lord and Savior."[4]

The Statement of Fundamental Truths of the Assemblies of God echoes this: "Salvation is received through repentance toward God and faith toward our Lord Jesus Christ. By the washing of regeneration and renewing of the Holy Spirit, being justified by grace through faith, man becomes an heir of God, according to the hope of eternal life."[5]

Repentance and faith began our life with Jesus. They are to remain hallmarks of our walk with Him. Theologian Wayne Grudem explains, "Although it is true that *initial* saving faith and *initial* repentance occur only once in our lives, and when they occur they constitute true conversion, nonetheless, the heart attitudes of repentance and faith only begin at conversion. These same attitudes should continue throughout the course of our Christian lives. Each day there should be heartfelt repentance for sins that we have committed, and faith in Christ to provide for our needs and to empower us to live the Christian life."[6]

Full repentance involves more than turning away from our sins. We repent—we turn away—from running our own lives, as well. When we come in repentance and faith to Christ He moves into the driver's seat. From then on He chooses our course. Elisabeth Elliot wrote pointedly of this surrender of will: "'Follow You, Lord? Well, yes, sure—but let me have a little input, won't You, about where we're going?' Nothing could be further from the spirit of the Gospel... Jesus Christ is Savior because He is Lord. He is Lord because He is Savior. I cannot be saved from my sins unless I am also saved from myself, so Christ must be 'commanding officer' in my life."[7]

It's the obvious response to Jesus—He is the Lord, I am His servant. Oswald Chambers, whose *My Utmost for His Highest* perennially remains in the top tier of daily devotionals, wrote, "When His life has been created in me by His Redemption, I instantly recognize His right to absolute authority over me."[8]

We've all heard it—*all you have to do is receive Jesus*. That is wonderfully true but receiving Christ doesn't mean just a nod of appreciation that He died for you. It means you bow before Him as your new, from-this-day-forward-king. You're not only receiving a gift, you're receiving God in the person of Jesus Christ. God the Son is to be acknowledged as your sovereign as well as your Savior. John 1:12 is one of the greatest assurances for believers in all the Scriptures. "But as many as received Him, to them He gave the right to become children of God, to those who believe in His name." The word *receive* in the original language is *lambano*. It carries the idea of grabbing hold with intensity and never letting go. Greek scholars describe the intent of this word and its usage in this verse: "*Receive someone* in the sense of recognizing his authority."[9] *To believe* in His name literally means to trust into His name. So when we receive Jesus it means we're *all in* with Him. A faithful rendering of this verse could read, "To as many as embraced Him and His authority, to those He gave authority to become children of God, to those who are all in, trusting into His name."

It's the very reason Jesus died and rose again, according to Paul. "For to this end Christ died and rose and lived again, that He might be Lord of both the dead and living" (Ro. 14:9). We do not "make" Jesus Lord. He is Lord and we're to acknowledge Him as such. This new life in Christ isn't only about cleansing, it's also about control. Who will be in charge of your life? According to theologian Larry Hart, "Authentic Christian faith always entails this confession of Jesus Christ: *My Lord and my God!*"[10]

There are some who counter that "lordship salvation," as they call it, somehow diminishes the singular role of God's grace in our salvation. Yet few if any have ever preached a purer, stronger message of saving grace than Charles Spurgeon. Here is Spurgeon's assessment of how we are to come to Jesus: "I cannot conceive for anyone to truly receive Christ as Savior and yet not to receive Him as Lord. One of the first instincts of a redeemed soul is to fall at the feet of the Savior and gratefully and adoringly to cry, 'Blessed Master, bought with Your precious blood, I acknowledge that I am Yours—Yours only, Yours wholly, Yours forever! Lord, what will You have me to do?' A man that is really saved by Grace does not need to be told that he is under solemn obligations to serve Christ—the new life within him tells him that. Instead of regarding it as a burden, he gladly surrenders himself—body, soul, and spirit, to the Lord that has redeemed him, reckoning this to be his reasonable service."[11]

This is why Paul appealed to all believers, "I urge you therefore, brothers, by the mercies of God, that you present your bodies as a living sacrifice, holy, and acceptable to God, which is your reasonable service of worship" (Ro. 12:1, MEV). The Greek word translated *reasonable* is *logikos*, from which we get the English word *logical*. The rational response to His great love is to yield everything to Him in grateful service. True, intelligent worship will always place us at the feet of Jesus, King of kings and Lord of lords.

"God exalted this man to His right hand as ruler and Savior" (Ac.5:31, HCSB). If this is the position the Father gives to Jesus it is the position we should give to Jesus. He is both Savior and ruler. Jesus is in charge. This is true kingdom life. Wherever Jesus truly rules, there is the kingdom of God. His kingdom dynamics kick in. Love kicks in and we start longing to see others experience His love.

THE STANDARD OF LOVE

People never forget love in action, especially in a time of crisis. I remember years ago visiting Westminster Hall, the great Methodist edifice in central London. This beautiful old structure was turned into a bomb shelter during World War II. For many harrowing nights the gallant pastor of the church, W.E. Sangster, ministered to the frightened masses who crowded into the underground halls. On Sundays he would preach in the upstairs auditorium.

Now, years after Sangster's death, I was walking through the building, admiring a life-sized statue of John Wesley, and drinking in the history of the place. I noticed a little bookstall in the corner of the main lobby, and behind the stall was a pleasant little man. His plaid shirt contrasted sharply with his tie that must have been a good six inches wide. Stuck prominently on the tie was a red sticker: "Smile! God loves you."

We chatted for a couple of minutes. Then I remarked, "This is where Sangster pastored, isn't it?"

Immediately a single tear began sliding down the old gentleman's cheek. "You couldn't fit all the people in here to hear him preach," he replied with a faraway gaze. "We'll never forget him."

Your kindness will live longer than you will. And people today are desperate for it. A word. A prayer. A call. A touch. The need for the ministry of apologetics (a rational defense of the gospel) cannot be overstated. But the ultimate apologetic for the gospel is the love of God flowing out of us, even toward—especially toward—our enemies. Robert Speer observed, "The Gospel came as a clear message to man's intelligence, and no small part of its power as it set out across the world was its positive answer to the age-old questions of men's minds about God and life and destiny. But it had an equal element of power in its charity and love."[12]

The apostle Paul laid out the clear standard for our conduct as gospel-carriers. "As the elect of God, holy and beloved, put on tender mercies, kindness, humility, meekness, longsuffering; bearing with one another, and forgiving one another, if anyone has a complaint against another; even as Christ forgave you, so you also must do. But above all these things put on love" (Col. 3:12-14). We're to wear God's love like a garment. It is the "finishing touch" of our character and conduct.

Paul delineates what it looks like to wear God's love. Our lives will be marked by kindness, forgiveness, and forbearance. It looks a lot like Jesus, doesn't it? That's because it is Jesus. His life, His love within us starts oozing out. "The love of God has been poured out in our hearts by the Holy Spirit" (Ro. 5:5). Here are three ways among many we can wear God's love.

We wear God's love when we share the gospel. The best way to wear God's love is to share the gospel with those who need its life-giving message. "The love of Jesus Christ for us, and our love for Him, compel us to tell others about Him," wrote Bill Bright. "Helping to fulfill Christ's Great Commission is both a duty and a privilege. We share because we love Christ. We share because He loves us. We tell others because we want to honor and obey Him. We tell them because He gives us a special quality of love for them."[13]

Fanny Crosby was blind from early childhood. Yet she refused to let her blindness define her. She became one of the most prolific writers of hymns and gospel songs in church history. Often this blind little lady (famous to almost everyone but herself) would stand on the street corner handing out gospel tracts to anyone who would take them. Who knows how many people we will meet in heaven because of her faithful witness for Christ? Her songs were like a gushing fountain, dispensing the living water to multitudes. Fanny modeled this standard of love, tying kindness to our sharing of the gospel. Fanny's call to urgent gospel witness pulsates through her song, "Rescue the Perishing." Once she was asked which of her thousands of verses of song she considered her best. Pausing to reflect, this small giant of a saint replied, "I think it's this one:"

> *Down in the human heart, crushed by the Tempter,*
> *Feelings lie buried that grace can restore.*
> *Touched by a loving heart, wakened by kindness,*
> *Chords that were broken will vibrate once more.*

Rescue the perishing; care for the dying.
Jesus is merciful; Jesus will save.[14]

We wear God's love when we forgive. Life sees to it that we have plenty of opportunities to forgive others. Because of deep wounds and severe injustices many people are drenched in bitterness. There's no denying the legitimacy of their reasons for pain. At the same time, we all have our stories of injustice to tell. It's part of living in a fallen world. But refusing to forgive carries consequences.

Unforgiveness is extremely costly. In fact, one might say it is a "luxury item." Perhaps that is why some people seem to luxuriate in it, not stopping to realize that they will pay for it in long, expensive installments. Part of that payment is that unforgiveness forces one's point of reference for life to always be in the past. It's like a ball and chain that prevents you from running toward the future. God doesn't want your life to literally be eaten away by unforgiveness.

I'm not saying unilateral forgiveness is easy. But it is liberating. And you can do it. We're able to forgive because we've been forgiven. God's grace that forgave our offenses against Him now becomes the grace we draw on to forgive those who've offended us. Here again we see the gospel's might on display. "Be kind to one another, tenderhearted, forgiving one another, even as God in Christ forgave you" (Eph. 4:32).

We wear God's love when we put the interests of Christ's kingdom and the interests of others above our own. In Sunday school when I was growing up I was often reminded, "Jesus-Others-and You. What a wonderful way to spell joy!" How simple, and how simply vital to get the order right. Yet the apostle Paul cautions us that "in the last days, perilous times will come: for men will be lovers of themselves" (2 Tim. 3:1-2). I don't think there's ever been a time in history when the cult of self has been on such blatant display as today.

"Be clothed with humility," Peter wrote, "for 'God resists the proud, but gives grace to the humble'" (1 Pet. 5:5). Just as we intentionally put on love, we must specifically put on humility. Humility begins by humbling ourselves before the Lord. That's one reason I've gone back to kneeling in prayer whenever possible. It's a physical gesture whereby I reaffirm the true order of things. As I bow before Him I'm acknowledging, "You are God. I am not. You are in charge. I am not. You are the Lord. I am Your servant as well as Your son."

We hear a lot about "self-fulfillment," "self-realization," and "self-actualization." For many, they themselves are the hub of all that matters, the sun around which everything in their little self-crafted universe orbits. It wasn't that long ago that Christians spoke in terms of "self-sacrifice," and "self-denial." Isn't it interesting? Those whose focus was Jesus and others instead of themselves ended up being a lot more self-fulfilled and self-actualized than most people today.

Paul wrote an extended passage about living in deference to others. Five times in 1 Corinthians 9 Paul said he surrendered his natural proclivities in order to give the gospel more favorable leverage among those who didn't know Christ. "I have made myself a servant to all, that I might win more of them… I do it all for the sake of the gospel, that I might share with them in its blessings" (1 Cor. 9:19, 23, ESV).

Loving God, loving others. According to Jesus, pleasing God boils down to this. "'You shall love the Lord your God with all your heart, with all your soul, with all your mind, and with all your strength.' This is the first commandment. And the second, like it, is this, 'You shall love your neighbor as yourself.'" (Mk. 12:30-31).

"But that's not natural," you may say. You've got that right. It's supernatural. As those who know Jesus Christ, we're invited—no, commanded—to draw on His love and park our lives there. "Make yourselves at home in my love" (Jn. 15:9, MSG).

THE STANDARD OF INTEGRITY

As never before, the whole world is watching to see if Christians' lives match their words. Much of the anger against us today is a reaction to our duplicity. Devout Muslims decry our immorality, secularists scorn our hypocrisy and atheists smirk at our lack of commitment.

But why should they care? Why should those who don't believe the gospel care whether we live up to our profession? The answer is tucked away in the story of Jonah's flight away from his missionary call. While the prophet slept, God judged his disobedience with a violent storm. The sailors cried out to their false gods to save them but to no avail. Finally, Jonah was shaken awake and he confessed to those on board, "I know that this great tempest is because of me" (Jon. 1:12).

Suddenly a group of cursing sailors became holiness preachers, preaching to the backslidden preacher! "Why have you done this?" they confronted Jonah. "For the men knew that he fled from the presence of the Lord" (v. 10). Could it be that even a pagan world somehow knows that at least part of the reason for their "tempest" is our disobedience? Do they somehow sense that *our* rebellion is imperiling *them*? They make no profession of righteousness, but we do. They have no gospel mandate, but we do. And when we run from our assignment our sin endangers everybody.

Our failure to give the gospel its best possible hearing cannot be laid at the feet of radical Muslims, belligerent governments, or blaspheming atheists. The greatest impediment to the reception of the gospel in our day is our own carnality! As Billy Graham observed, "The gospel must be communicated not only by our lips but by our lives. This is a visual proof that the message we preach can actually change lives."[15]

If your brand of grace doesn't lead to a holy life, you didn't get the real deal. Grace isn't disgrace. True grace produces lives that adorn the gospel. Timothy Keller notes, "We are saved by faith alone, but not by a faith that remains alone. True faith will always produce a changed life."[16] If there is no life change in someone who claims he is a Christian, this is cause not just for concern but alarm. "Examine yourselves to see whether you are in the faith; test yourselves. Do you not realize that Christ Jesus is in you—unless, of course, you fail the test?" (2 Cor.13:5, NIV).

Over the last several decades the church has been enmeshed in one infamous scandal after another. There is, however, a scandal for which we should be famous. It is the scandal we should gladly own and never avoid. It is the scandal of Christ and His cross.

Tragically, Christians have been involved in all the wrong scandals. I pray that in the future the church will be identified with the *right* scandal—our loyalty to and identity with Jesus Christ and Him crucified. If we are going to be "nailed" as scandalous, this is where we must take the nails. Jesus is a "stone of stumbling" and a "rock of offense." The cross and the person of Christ literally trip people up who are going their own, defiant way. The offense of the cross is that it is a scandalous line of demarcation, cleaving all humanity into disciples or opponents. Jesus is opposed—often violently opposed—by those He and His cross offend. But it is our honor, never our shame, to stand with Him. This "rock of offense" for us has become the "chief cornerstone," the very foundation stone of our faith (1 Pet. 2:7-8).

Notice the profound difference: Unrighteous scandals bring shame. This scandal delivers from shame. "Behold, I lay in Zion a stumbling stone and rock of offense [*skandalon* in Greek], and whoever believes on Him will not be put to shame" (Ro. 9:33). This cross—this sacrifice—that is so repugnant to others is attractive and precious to us who believe. While the cross makes some stumble, it is our boast and glory. "May I never boast except in the cross of our Lord Jesus Christ, through which the world has been crucified to me, and I to the world" (Gal. 6:14).

The word *integrity* comes from the mathematics term *integer*. As you probably recall from school days, an integer is a whole number. It isn't split or fractioned. In the same way, a person of integrity is a whole person. The public persona is a match with the private person. There is no duplicity. If there is any degree of difference between who we are perceived to be and who we really are, to that degree we have lost integrity, wholeness. This sets the stage for loss of trust. And when trust in the messenger is compromised the message is often compromised, as well. Those who claim allegiance to Christ "must show themselves to be entirely trustworthy. In this way they will make people want to believe in our Savior and God" (Titus 2:10, TLB).

Our salvation has nothing to do with our works. Jesus forever finished the work of redemption on the cross. There is great liberty in the gospel. But our freedom should never be construed as license for unrighteous living. That's not what we've been made for. It's not what we've been re-made for. Instead we've been "created in Christ Jesus for good works, which God prepared beforehand that we should walk in them" (Eph. 2:10). We are new creations in Christ Jesus. "We are His *workmanship*" (Eph. 2:10, italics added). The original Greek word is *poema*. God is writing something beautiful through our lives.

So can you be a Christian and still sin? The overwhelming evidence says yes. We continue to "fall short of the glory of God" (Ro. 3:23). But, as a true follower of Jesus, you cannot sin and not grieve. We grieve knowing that we have grieved the tender Holy Spirit who lives within us. The way back to full fellowship with the Lord is to come clean before Him in quick confession and full repentance. Then, "He is faithful and just to forgive us our sins and to cleanse us from all unrighteousness" (1 Jn. 1:9).

As Matt Chandler says, "Get *over* yourself. You were saved by grace alone through faith alone. Therefore, God gets all the glory alone. And when you understand this one basic issue, you'll stop going into you and start going into the Lord—just laying out all the smelly, rotten groceries, shaking all the stuff out of your pockets, bringing it all out into the open, and saying, 'Here, would You please get rid of this for me?'"[17]

"He saved us and called us to a holy life—not because of anything we have done but because of his own purpose and grace. This grace was given us in Christ Jesus before the beginning of time, but it has now been revealed through the appearing of our Savior, Christ Jesus, who has destroyed death and has brought life and immortality to light through the gospel" (2 Tim. 1:9-10, NIV).

The Standard of Boldness

Wherever disaster strikes in the world Christians should be the first responders. And we are. It is Christian relief teams who often arrive long before government help and almost always before help from any other religious group. Observers are forced to ask, "Why are Christians most often the first on the scene when there is large-scale human need?" It's because our instinctive, compassionate aid for the suffering isn't grounded in politics, it's grounded in theology.

The reasons behind Christians' rapid response and the slow response of others (if they respond at all) are embedded in the beliefs of major world religions. If, for instance, a tsunami occurs, in all likelihood Christians will arrive well before relief teams representing the same religion as those affected by the disaster. Some may be stymied from offering aid even to those of their same faith because they think their help could be an *interference*. In their belief system the Almighty has allowed this disaster to come upon them. And one dare not interfere with the will of the Almighty. Those of yet another religion may be prevented from helping because they think their help could be an *interruption*.

In the cycle of life fate or karma has dealt a harsh blow. Their religion strongly infers this has happened to teach those affected some important lesson. Therefore, one should not bring aid or comfort because that would interrupt the consequences of their determined fate.[18]

As Christians, however, we believe our ministry to those in need is neither interference in some predestined outcome nor interruption in some fatalistic cycle. Rather, based on Scripture, we believe in *intervention*. This is what God did for us in sending Jesus. We too were desperate. We remember what it was like to be those "having no hope and without God in the world." Then God intervened! "But now in Christ Jesus you who once were far off have been brought near by the blood of Christ" (Eph. 2:12-13).

Now He sends us in Christ's behalf as interventionists to bring hope in the midst of pain. The world is a much better place because a gospel-driven William Wilberforce intervened to outlaw slave trafficking, because a gospel-driven David Livingstone intervened to bring medicine and commerce to disease-riddled central Africa, and because a gospel-driven Amy Carmichael intervened to stop child prostitution that functioned under the wicked guise of religious ritual.

But a life given to intervention, especially when such intervention may not be wanted (at least initially), requires boldness and courage. How can we acquire boldness? The same way the early Christians got it. They asked for it. "Grant to Your servants that with all boldness they may speak Your word" (Ac. 4:29). They received exactly what they requested. "And they were all filled with the Holy Spirit, and they spoke the word of God with boldness" (Ac. 4:31).

We live in a time of seething anger. Civil discourse is almost a thing of the past. In times like these it's crucial to remember there's a difference, an important difference, between being bold and being rude. We can share the gospel forcefully without being intentionally abrasive. Our assignment is to be winsome ambassadors of the truth. Our call as gospel carriers is to exhibit boldness without brashness, anointing without arrogance, and power without pride. As Chuck Swindoll admonishes, "Let people be offended by the message of the cross, not by the messengers of the cross."[19]

Because Jesus has broken through the barrier, we now have *boldness in praying*. In Christ, "we have boldness and access with confidence through faith in Him" (Eph. 3:11-12). Now we have a passkey to the very control center of the universe! "Let us therefore come boldly to the throne of grace, that we may obtain mercy and find grace to help in time of need" (Heb. 4:16).

Because of Jesus we can have *boldness in proclaiming*. Living under the gospel's standard means we follow the truth, speak the truth, and call people to the truth. Again, this requires boldness. From a prison cell Paul asked for prayer "that I may open my mouth boldly to make known the mystery of the gospel, for which I am an ambassador in chains; that in it I may speak boldly, as I ought to speak" (Eph. 6:19-20). His prayer was answered. Five times in Acts it says Paul boldly preached the gospel (9:27; 9:29; 14:3; 18:26; 19:8).

Because of Jesus we can have *boldness in persecution*. Paul was shipwrecked, flogged, spat on, imprisoned often, and his motives were impugned (by "good Christian people"). He lived under constant threat of murder and was beaten three times within an inch of his life—all for the sake of the gospel. He serves as a triumphant model for the millions of Christian believers today who pay a substantial price for their loyalty to Jesus.

Assessing all he had suffered for the testimony of Jesus Paul concluded, "Our light and momentary troubles are achieving for us an eternal glory that far outweighs them all" (2 Cor. 4:17, NIV). Since Jesus has always promised to be with us "we may boldly say: 'The Lord is my helper; I will not fear. What can man do to me?'" (Heb. 13:6).

Trusting His enabling grace our lives are to be marked both by courtesy and courage, by civility and holy boldness. When fierce winds oppose us our confidence in the gospel anchors our souls. "We who have fled to Him for refuge can take new courage, for we can hold on to His promise with confidence. This confidence is like a strong and trustworthy anchor for our souls" (Hebrews 6:18-19 NLT).

WHAT KIND OF PEOPLE?

God spoke to my heart early one morning. I was shaving with a dull blade and suddenly I heard in my spirit, "You're living below your privileges."

A brief background. Several months prior I had signed up for those inexpensive but good razor blades to be sent to me by mail. For decades I'd conditioned myself to use each blade for a long, long time—especially as blades kept rising in cost. Well, now I have several packs of unused, sharp blades. A new set of blades is mailed to me each month. I need to recondition my thinking. I'm not "blade poor" anymore. I don't have to shave with dull blades ever again! In fact, I have more than enough sharp, new blades. That morning I was shaving below my privileges and my provision.

It's a simple illustration but it spotlights a vital truth. So often we live below the privileges and provisions the gospel brings. "His divine power has given to us all things that pertain to life and godliness, through the knowledge of Him" (2 Pet. 1:3). All we need for life, all we need for godliness we already have through Christ! Further, we have been given "exceedingly great and precious promises, that through these you may be partakers of the divine nature" (vs.4).

The Father gave His Son. Jesus gave His life. The Spirit gives His gifts. God "has blessed us with every spiritual blessing in the heavenly places in Christ" (Eph. 1:3). Are you living below your privileges?

We are *sons* of God through faith in Christ (Jn. 1:12). We are *heirs* of an eternal kingdom (Ro. 8:17; Eph. 3:6). We are *ambassadors* for an eternal Sovereign (2 Cor. 5:20). To live below our privileges in Christ dishonors our Father. Much of our lack is self-imposed. Only when we live in the benefits of our secure, exalted position are we inclined to be lavish in our generosity. This isn't about money. It's about identity. How do you see yourself? Your answer will in large part determine how you view life.

When we realize the unending resources we have in the gospel we begin to live as Covenant people have always been commissioned to live. We are "blessed—to be a blessing—to all the nations of the earth" (Gen. 12:1-3; Psa. 67:1-2). When I shared this with my sister she responded with a witty smile, "This is cutting edge theology!"

As gospel carriers let's live in, let's *swim* in the privileges we have in Jesus Christ. Then, may we sense our responsibility to adorn the gospel by lives lived solely for Jesus' honor. The best way to thank Him for such a great salvation is, by His grace, to exhibit lives worthy of the gospel. And it is His life in us that enables us to do just that. It's our response of love to His love for us. "The love of Christ for us as revealed in the gospel will help us want to change for the right reason," writes Jerry Bridges. "God wants us to desire to do what is our duty to do, and only the gospel will produce that desire."[20]

In light of God's coming judgment of the world's unrighteousness Peter asks, "What kind of people ought you to be? You ought to live holy and godly lives" (2 Pet. 3:11). We acknowledge that this gospel treasure is housed in jars of clay (2 Cor. 4:7, NIV). In our human frailties we know our potential to do great damage to the message of Christ. What an indictment: "The name of God is blasphemed among the Gentiles *because of you*" (Ro. 2:24, italics added). But we also know that obedience to Christ can draw many people to Him: "They glorified God *because of me*" (Gal. 1:24, ESV, italics added). How will the gospel fare because of you?

Let's keep growing in grace and in the knowledge of Jesus (2 Pet. 3:18). Like dead leaves old habits are pushed off by new, growing life. This pulsating, new life of Christ was described by Scottish preacher Thomas Chalmers as "the expulsive power of a new affection."[21] The old, dead life is pushed off and pushed away by the new life. We begin to discover the great "open secret" that changed missionary Hudson Taylor and sent His fruitfulness into overdrive. It is "the simple, profound secret of drawing for every need, temporal or spiritual, upon 'the fathomless wealth of Christ.'"[22]

> How will the gospel fare because of you?

"Let your bearing toward one another arise out of your life in Christ Jesus," Paul wrote to Philippian believers (Phil. 2:5, NEB). Jesus Himself is the standard and, as His followers, we will one day answer to Him for our lives.[23] Harry Reeder counsels young Christ-followers, "Young Christian, the world despises the gospel in its simplicity and disdains the vessels entrusted to carry and proclaim it. But there is power under the hood. Live the gospel, believe and preach the whole gospel—the gospel blessings that declare who you are in Christ, the gospel imperatives that call you to your new life for Christ. The gospel transforms the hearts, minds, and wills of sinners. Thankfully, it continues to transform mine. Preach to yourself, to each other, and to the lost, and know the joys of the gospel-driven life."[24] Those who sell out for Jesus will never lack for adventure. Gospel carriers often feel the scorn of enemies, the thanks of believers, the smile of God, the joy of the Lord, and the applause of heaven—all at the same time!

God grant that we "walk worthy of the Lord, fully pleasing Him, being fruitful in every good work and increasing in the knowledge of God" (Col. 1:10). I want to see Jesus personally

Those who sell out for Jesus will never lack for adventure.

known, ardently loved, lavishly worshiped, and radically obeyed. I don't want my life to prevent others from coming to Jesus. I want my life to propel people toward Him.

By His grace and goodness I've been preaching the gospel for half a century, starting as a teenager. I've never gotten over the wonder of it. Just to think that we are identified with Jesus at this crucial juncture in history; that we bear His name, and represent His cause in the world. How amazing. How focusing. How humbling. "Who is sufficient for these things? ...Not that we are sufficient in ourselves to claim anything as coming from us, but our sufficiency is from God, who has made us competent to be ministers of the new covenant" (2 Cor. 2:16; 3:5-6, ESV).

What I've tried to say in this chapter can be summed up in this phrase:

Jesus paid it all;
All to Him I owe.[25]

Jesus paid it all—that's the gospel. *All to Him I owe*—that's the gospel's standard. "Now may the God of peace make you holy in every way, and may your whole spirit and soul and body be kept blameless until our Lord Jesus Christ comes again. God will make this happen, for he who calls you is faithful" (1 Thess. 5:23-24, NLT).

SIX

THE GOSPEL—
COMMITTED TO ITS TRUTH

But we did not give and submit to these people even for an hour, so that the truth of the gospel would be preserved for you.

2 Corinthians 2:5, HCSB

The truth claims of Christianity, by their very particularity and exclusivity, are inherently offensive to those who would demand some other gospel.

Albert Mohler
Culture Shift

We are authorized to proclaim the gospel. We are not authorized to amend it.

The previous chapter addressed how we are to live as gospel carriers. This chapter is a call to commit to the truth of the un-amended, full strength gospel of the Lord Jesus Christ. No wonder Paul counseled his young protege, Timothy, "Watch your life and doctrine closely. Persevere in them, because if you do, you will save both yourself and your hearers" (1 Tim. 4:16, NIV). What great counsel: Watch how you live. Watch what you believe.

"Our gospel did not come to you in word only," Paul noted, "but also in power, and in the Holy Spirit and in much confidence, as you know what kind of men we were among you for your sake" (1 Thess. 1:5). When we're empowered by God's Spirit, confident in the gospel, and living out the gospel's standard as citizens of

We are authorized to proclaim the gospel. We are not authorized to amend it.

God's kingdom, amazing things happen. Life pulsates with adventure as we watch the gospel's supernatural qualities on display in lives transformed by its power.

Since the church's earliest days the gospel has contended with detractors. These opponents have proffered a host of alternatives to the simple good news of Jesus Christ. Millions have been led down dark, dead-end paths by those purporting some enlightened way that excludes the light of the world. In the end these alternate avenues with substitute saviors at best bring only partial solutions and no regeneration. These counterfeit "gospels" also bring bitter disappointment. "There is a way that seems right to a man, but its end is the way of death" (Prov. 14:12).

Still, many ascribe to some alternative "good news" that precludes the lordship of Christ. Under whatever pretext people find ways to declare, "We will not have this man to reign over us" (Lu. 19:14). But defying the biblical gospel has its consequences, in this life and the next. "They perish because they refused to love the truth and so be saved. For this reason God sends them a powerful delusion so that they will believe the lie" (2 Thess. 2:10-11).

Among the gospel's assailants today are an array of distortions, diversions, and outright assaults. In the end, God's truth triumphs. The gospel will ultimately win over all who would contest its supreme authority. As Dale Evrist asserts, "The gospel of Jesus Christ is the only message that can tell you what's wrong with you and also tell you how to make it right."[1]

DISTORTIONS

"The problem all around us is the reality of adjusted gospels," writes Albert Mohler, "ranging from the seductively revised to the blatantly false."[2]

Several times the apostle Paul warned of those who tout "another Jesus" and "a different gospel" (2 Cor. 11:4). He reserved his most stinging rebuke for anyone who dared to mess with the gospel. "Evidently some people are throwing you into confusion and are trying to pervert the gospel of Christ. But even if we or an angel from heaven should preach a gospel other than the one we preached to you, let them be under God's curse! As we have already said, so now I say again: If anybody is preaching to you a gospel other than what you accepted, let them be under God's curse!" (Gal. 1:7-9).

This is the most blistering denunciation found in any of Paul's letters. He says it twice for double emphasis. And he makes no exemptions. Allow me to paraphrase but remain true to the text. "I don't care who it is," Paul was saying. "Even if I come at a later date with some distortion to the gospel you have received already from me, let *me* be under God's curse! Not only that, I don't care if it's an angel, not a fallen angel but an angel straight from heaven, if he carries a message that distorts the gospel you have received, let the *angel* be under God's curse!"

I'd say that's Exhibit A of how tenacious we need to be in protecting the gospel of Jesus Christ. Talk about a deep sense of stewardship. Paul knew he was *entrusted* with the gospel. Its purity and simplicity must be guarded at all costs. Now we too have been entrusted with the treasure of God's good news. It is our privilege and holy duty to both protect it and proclaim it no matter the cost.

My generation of preachers will surely give an account for the largescale erosion that has happened on our watch. Theological reductionism is now rampant. This dumbing down of biblical truth has spawned hazy beliefs that are supported more by soundbites than by Scripture. May God forgive some preachers for contributing to this doctrinal malaise instead of helping eradicate it. False ideologies rush in to fill the void a lack of clear gospel preaching creates.

Scott Hinkle speaks clearly to this: "Vague Christian teaching that does not specifically include the gospel cannot lead to spiritual regeneration. We have no choice but to stay the course of Scripture if we want to see people saved. Though some people might say that sounds narrow-minded, it is nonetheless biblically true. We can preach about power, love, money, health, and a litany of other good, even vital, matters of life. But according to Romans 10:14 and other examples from the New Testament, without the preaching of the gospel there can be no salvation, period."[3] The word must come first. The gospel must be foremost. "For I delivered to you as of first importance what I also received: that Christ died for our sins in accordance with the Scriptures, that he was buried, that he was raised on the third day in accordance with the Scriptures" (1 Cor. 15:3-4, ESV).

Spiritual feelings are a response to our faith and our faith is embedded in historical facts, particularly the death and resurrection of Jesus. We must be vigilant to keep the *logos*—the word—of the gospel paramount. This in no way negates or even diminishes the experiential nature of our faith and our walk with Jesus. Make no mistake, biblical Christianity is not merely a mental assertion to true postulates. We should feel it. After all, at the core of all this is a *relationship* with the Father through the Son activated by the Spirit. But this relationship, though real and personal, rests on facts of history and truths of Scripture. It stands in juxtaposition to the ambiguous spirituality so popular today. Our love for Jesus is tethered to verifiable truth.

Scripture exhorts us to "contend earnestly for the faith which was once for all delivered to the saints" (Jude 3). *The Message* rendering of this verse is powerful: "Fight with everything you have in you for this faith entrusted to us as a gift to guard and cherish." While distortions of the gospel are many, let me mention just a few of the more glaring warps of the genuine gospel message.

There are, for instance, some who assert that since Jesus has covered all our sins we are now free from any restraints whatsoever. Such teaching has little use for the moral law God established for all human behavior. It is guised under a teaching of grace. In fact, as stated in the previous chapter, this isn't true grace, it's disgrace. Some of those who oppose this aberration (as I do) have termed such teaching "hyper-grace." Personally I think it's impossible to over-extol the grace of God. Therefore, I don't really like the term "hyper-grace." The theological term is *antinomianism*.[4] We must never forget that God's amazing grace is freely dispensed not to sinners in general but to *repentant* sinners. And while it is thankfully true that God's grace does indeed cover our sins, it is equally true that we will give an account of our post-conversion lives at the Judgment Seat of Christ (Ro. 14:10, 2 Cor. 5:10). This sobering truth is a built-in prompt to godly living.

Swinging the pendulum to the other side, there are others who espouse highly moral lives, "doing what God wants," with little or no mention of the transformation wrought by a spiritual rebirth. This is placing law before grace and even above grace. The early church dealt head-on with this false gospel of "works righteousness." This was the specific problem Paul addressed in his letter to the Galatians. This "grace plus" message of legalism, also called *moralism*, has been an incessant challenge to the purity of the gospel. And frankly, it doesn't work. Even if lives look better on the outside the inner person remains unchanged.

Paul reprimanded some believers in Rome for causing God's name to be mocked among unbelievers (Ro. 2:24). They were guilty of both loose lives *and* legalism. While they paid lip service to God's law, they dishonored Him by not living up to the gospel's standard. Then as now, legalism had the reverse effect of unholiness instead of holiness. This is because holiness of heart comes not by law but by grace. Love for the Lord, not legalism and the law, produces attractive holiness. As Al Mohler reminds us, "We are justified by faith *alone,* saved by grace *alone,* and redeemed from our sin by Christ *alone.* Moralism produces sinners who are (potentially) better behaved. The Gospel of Christ transforms sinners into sons and daughters of God."[5]

Another distortion of the gospel asserts that *man is basically good.* The "politically correct" climate so rampant today applauds this gospel-imposter. Scripture describes our true condition: "Surely I was sinful at birth, sinful from the time my mother conceived me" (Psa. 51:5, NIV). Yet these days the ultimate "sin" is making anyone feel badly about his behavior.

I want to be clear. We are not the Holy Spirit. It is not our job to bring conviction to anyone. That's the Spirit's work. But to reduce blatant transgressions to "misjudgments" and "poor choices" is, as stated earlier, messing with the gospel. The Holy Spirit convicts us of our sins, not to condemn us but as the precursor to our condemnation being removed by the gospel. Only those convicted of sin will then repent of their sin. And only those who repent of sin can then embrace their Savior from sin and sin's outcomes. Scripture is clear that all people, including the most willful transgressors, are made in God's image. Therefore, all people are to be respected and valued. Beyond that, when the Holy Spirit activates God's compassion in us we see with God's eyes and we're enabled to love those whom others may loathe.

Humankind, the zenith of God's creation, made in His image, is also marred by sin. Yet today, from pundits to counselors to liberal theologians, many vehemently deny the obvious. As agnostic-turned-apologist Malcolm Muggeridge observed, "The depravity of man is at once the most empirically verifiable reality but at the same time the most intellectually resisted fact."[6] We are born with a proclivity to sin. Innately we are rebels against God. As the great lion Aslan, a type of Christ, says in C. S. Lewis' fourth *Chronicles of Narnia book, Prince Caspian,* "You come of the Lord Adam and the Lady Eve. And that is both honor enough to erect the head of the poorest beggar, and shame enough to bow the shoulders of the greatest emperor on earth."[7]

Lewis's balanced statement attests to both our dignity and our need. Being made in God's image we are creatures of unfathomable worth. Being heirs of Earth's first parents, we bear the shame of their rebellion against God as well as our own. Thus our great need for the gospel and our great need for Jesus.

Another popular distortion of the gospel can only be mentioned. *Syncretism* seeks to merge the biblical gospel with aspects of other religions. It is a toxic mix of truth with error. Again, this is not just a distortion of the gospel. It is a defilement and must be strongly rejected.

What some scornfully call *the prosperity gospel* must also be addressed, if only briefly. I've devoted an entire chapter to this multi-layered issue in *A Force in the Earth.*[8] Honestly, I take umbrage with this term. To merge "prosperity" and "gospel," whether used by proponents or opponents, creates a term that doesn't appear in Scripture. To keep the gospel untainted we are on safest ground when we only let biblical descriptives be aligned with the word *gospel*—such as *the gospel of the kingdom, the gospel of Jesus Christ,* and *the gospel of grace.*

Make no mistake, when people embrace the gospel their entire life is lifted. No believer in Jesus Christ need ever be impoverished mentally or spiritually. As a result of the gospel taking root one may not get a bigger lawn but the grass will be mowed. He may not get a nicer car but the car he has will be clean and maintained. When Jesus comes a sense of stewardship comes.

Having been freed to wholeness in Christ, it is reasonable to expect that the economic condition of believers will be positively affected by adherence to the gospel. At the same time, some preachers have defined prosperity solely in monetary terms, sometimes with little sensitivity to the plight of persecuted believers who are blacklisted in business in some parts of the world. Often Christians have been consigned to menial labor and unjust wages. Yet some teachers have supplanted the message of Christ's atoning work with the assurance of financial gain as the *primary* reason for embracing Christianity. Again, this goes beyond distortion and must be soundly withstood.

Paul warned Timothy to steer clear of those who equated godliness with financial gain. In his typical no-holds-barred fashion Paul said such teachers "were men of corrupt minds and destitute of the truth" (1 Tim. 6:5). As A. W. Tozer lamented decades ago, "God's gifts now take the place of God, and the whole course of nature is upset by the monstrous substitution."[9]

Let me say it again. Inherent in the gospel is upward mobility. God's heart is to bless His children in all dimensions of life. In fact, Scripture goes so far as to say that the Lord "delights in the prosperity of His servant" (Psa. 35:27, NASB). But this is *not* the central message of Scripture. It should never be allowed to supplant the Big Story of God sending His Son to redeem fallen humanity.

Any addition to the gospel of Jesus Christ, no matter how well intentioned, ultimately becomes a distracting, even dangerous barnacle. John Calvin felt we add to the gospel because we're dissatisfied with the beauty of the gospel itself. And this exposes a serious spiritual problem. He declared, "All those, then, who, not content with the gospel, patch it with something extraneous to it, detract from Christ's authority."[10] For the gospel to shine in its pristine grandeur it must stand alone. When the gospel, and only the gospel, is proclaimed it towers over all other messages and interests.

As stated often throughout this book, there is only one, all-sufficient gospel. Jack Hayford concurs, stating, "There is no gospel other than the gospel of the kingdom of God (or "of heaven"; Matt. 3:2; 4:17; Acts 28:23; Gal. 1:8-9). The gospel of the kingdom is the same as the gospel of Jesus Christ. Jesus Himself used the former expression frequently, while His followers rightly saw in Jesus both the coming of God's kingdom and the place of Jesus as King of the kingdom. Within a short time, the revelation of Jesus as Lord and Christ turned the popular way of referring to God's gospel toward the focus most familiar to us: 'the gospel of Jesus Christ.'"[11]

DIVERSIONS

Not only are we challenged with distortions of the true gospel, we also are tugged away from the gospel as the center by diversions. I'll mention just two.

There's a lot of fatigue among Christians. This has contributed to an emerging new category of Christians that is causing serious concern for the church's future—the *"Dones."* The Dones are the growing number of people, now recognized statistically, who are simply done with church. They seldom if ever attend church services.[12] Although they haven't defected from the faith, evangelism is no longer a priority. They've simply checked out of church involvement. Their emphasis has shifted from service to God and others to their own renewal and recreation. Regrettably, this signals that a growing percentage of potential gospel carriers are taking themselves out of the lineup.

In my opinion, although their love for God may remain strong most of the Dones have succumbed to the spirit of the times. James Emery White addresses this "me first" lifestyle: "We lose the vision God could give us of our world and our place in it. Too quickly, and often without struggle, we trade making history for making money, substitute building a life with building a career and sacrifice living for God with living for the weekend.... We become saved, but not seized; delivered, but not driven."[13] The only hope of re-engaging this much needed group is to reintroduce them to the gospel's grandeur. We must freshly appeal to them to live large for Jesus Christ.

On the other hand there is another influential group who, unlike the Dones, are strongly involved in ministry. Yet often with noble intentions they *replace the primacy of the gospel with social issues.* The gospel is put on the back burner, or even eventually discarded, while primary focus is given to addressing issues of social injustice.

Certainly any genuinely redeemed person will be sensitized to human need. Our humanitarian impulses will be augmented by the compassion of Christ's life within us. As mentioned previously we believe in intervening to help those in need. Work for social justice that is undergirded by the gospel is a demonstration of the kingdom of God. So of course we advocate for justice and the betterment of living conditions for all in need. We cannot obey Scripture without standing against and working against injustice and subjugation.

But we also cannot and must not supplant the gospel itself with social ministry. They should go together. Caring, loving acts done in Jesus' name are very effective precursors to evangelism. Our compassionate deeds open doors for the gospel. And social ministry will be the result of gospel proclamation. Any understanding of church history shows that. Wherever the gospel holds sway life gets better and living conditions improve. But social justice is not the gospel. It is the outgrowth of the gospel. It cannot be allowed to replace the gospel. Church history also shows that overriding the gospel with justice issues is not only a mistake, it curtails the impact of both. As Rob Hoskins writes, "Where we have let compassion vs. evangelism become an either/or proposition, we have failed in both… Spiritual justice, providing the biblical message of purpose and hope, along with the compassionate touch of the Savior, sets the stage for social justice."[14]

John Piper spoke eloquently and forcefully to this at the Third Lausanne Congress on World Evangelization in Capetown, South Africa:

"One truth is that when the gospel takes root in our souls it impels us out toward the alleviation of all unjust suffering in this age. That's what love does! The other truth is that when the gospel takes root in our souls it awakens us to the horrible reality of eternal suffering in hell, under the wrath of a just and omnipotent God. And it impels us to rescue the perishing and to warn people to flee from the wrath to come (1 Thessalonians 1:10).

"I plead with you. Don't choose between these two truths. Embrace them both. It doesn't mean we all spend our time in the same way. God forbid. But it means we let the Bible define reality and define love.

"Could Lausanne say—and could the Evangelical church say— we Christians care about all suffering, especially eternal suffering? I hope we can say that. But if we feel resistant to saying 'especially eternal suffering,' or if we feel resistant to saying 'we care about all suffering in this age,' then either we have a defective view of hell or a defective heart."

Any attempt at social justice minus the gospel would lead only to a man-made Utopia which would be short-lived and eventually riddled with injustice itself. Greg Gilbert warns, "Far too often among transformationalists, cultural redemption subtly becomes the great promise and point of the gospel—which of course means that the cross, deliberately or not, is pushed out of that position... The highest excitement and joy are ignited by the promise of a reformed culture rather than by the work of Christ on the cross.... The Bible's story line is said to pivot on the remaking of the world rather than on the substitutionary death of

If we truly want to see the social order redeemed and morality restored, we had better get back to seeing *people* redeemed and restored.

Jesus. And in the process, Christianity becomes less about grace and faith, and more a banal religion of 'Live like this, and we'll change the world.' That's not Christianity; it's moralism."[16]

God's mission is fueled by His love. That same healing fuel energizes and propels us into a broken world. If we truly want to see the social order redeemed and morality restored, we had better get back to seeing *people* redeemed and restored. Reborn people then become tools of grace to rebuild the world.

DIRECT ASSAULTS

Without question opposition to the gospel is intensifying in many parts of the world, including North America. Among the ideologies in the West that most adamantly oppose the gospel's advance, an unholy alliance has formed intertwining *atheism, secularism,* and *pluralism.* As Christians' evangelistic fervor has waned these forces have been invigorated. Secularism is sweeping through culture. Atheism, after decades of near silence, is now vocal and confrontational. Pluralism champions the libertine notion that everyone is free to espouse whatever beliefs they wish. Everyone, it seems, except evangelical Christians. The broad tolerance of pluralists often stops there.

Added to these assaults is the serious threat of *militant Islam.* Some Islamic groups brazenly declare their resolve to destroy the State of Israel and drive all Christians out of the Middle East. Many Christians have laid down their lives for the testimony of Jesus. Many others have become refugees, fleeing the ravages inflicted by militant Muslims.

But these atrocities are backfiring. Large sectors of Muslims are embarrassed and conflicted by the debased actions of some radical groups espousing Islam. Many Muslims are sickened by crucifixions and beheadings, rape of Christian women, and the senseless exile of families—all in the name of their religion. As a result increasing numbers of Muslims are open to other views and many are embracing the gospel of Jesus Christ. There is a raging battle within the vast numbers of Muslims for the soul of Islam. Will Islam accommodate twenty-first century realities and live peaceably with the rest of the world? Or will unreasoning jihadists become the dominant voices within Islam?

It needs to be noted that the increasing brutality of some sectors of Islam is not a sign of strength but weakness. Ideologies that are weak at their core often resort to violence for their propagation. Knowing they will not win in the arena of ideas, some extremist Muslims exert fierce coercion. These misguided terrorists are simply acting out their lostness. Their crimes against humanity mandate upon their own psyches that they shroud their atrocities in what they believe is a "holy cause."

We must remember that these terrorists, and all who ascribe to their misguided beliefs, are people for whom Jesus died. God loves them. They deserve the gospel and they clearly need its message of forgiveness and reconciliation. As followers of Jesus we have power to rise above the natural human inclinations of fear or recrimination. We can draw upon the very love of God that is activated in us by the Holy Spirit (Ro. 5:5; Gal. 5:22). Let's obey our Lord's teaching, "Love your enemies . . . and pray for those who spitefully use you and persecute you" (Matt. 5:14). We also must juxtapose our message, the gospel, in dramatic contrast to all hate-filled messages.

The news out of the Islamic World is not all bleak. More Muslims are coming to Christ than ever. Significant numbers are experiencing personal encounters with "the Man in white." God's love is breaking through all sorts of barriers to get the gospel to them.[17]

There is one more serious assault against the gospel in our day that must be addressed.

WILL EVERYONE GO TO HEAVEN?

William Booth, founder of The Salvation Army, served people trapped in the most degrading conditions. Yet he never suggested, as is often heard today, that desperate people are "already in hell." Booth believed in a real, eternal hell, and it drove him to rescue people from their current plight *and* from coming perdition. General Booth died in 1912. Shortly before his death he warned prophetically of what he saw coming to the church: ". . . religion without the Holy Ghost, Christianity without Christ, forgiveness without repentance, salvation without regeneration, politics without God, and heaven without hell."[18]

In today's theological fog Booth's ominous caveat is unfolding. Even some who claim to believe the Bible are having second thoughts about eternal judgment. Others have rejected the notion of judgment altogether. The name usually given this teaching is *universalism*.[19] Although there are several expressions of this doctrine, universalism is basically the belief that all people (possibly excluding the "Hitlers" of history) will be saved. According to this view, Jesus' death and resurrection automatically, or at least eventually, saves the whole human race. No personal repentance and faith in Christ are necessary for going to heaven. For universalists, our mission is reduced to announcing the "good news" to everyone that "you are already saved."

Universalism is an ancient heresy. It began in the Garden of Eden when the serpent told Adam and Eve, "You will not surely die" (Gen. 3:4). One of its first proponents was Origen of Alexandria. It was later roundly condemned by the church. Different shades of the teaching have periodically appeared, most notably in post-Reformation times in reaction to a strict doctrine of election, and in the nineteenth century when it was sometimes referred to as "the larger hope."

Scripture however leaves no doubt as to the final destiny of those without Christ. The Bible clearly describes a coming apocalypse "when the Lord Jesus is revealed from heaven with His mighty angels, in flaming fire taking vengeance on those who do not know God, and on those who do not obey the gospel of our Lord Jesus Christ. These shall be punished with everlasting destruction from the presence of the Lord and the glory of His power" (2 Thess. 1:7-9). There's no way to spin those verses to mean anything other than what they clearly say.

I admit this is difficult. It's wrenching to deal with the ramifications of friends, relatives, and the already disenfranchised being separated from God, and therefore separated from hope, for eternity. I believe God's love meant that this not be easy for us. We are to become uncomfortable enough to act, doing all we can to share the gospel with those who need Christ. "That's the whole point—we shouldn't just go on with life as usual," notes Francis Chan. "A sense of urgency over the reality of hell should recharge our passion for the gospel as it did for Paul, who 'knowing the fear of the Lord' persuaded people to believe (2 Cor. 5:11). We should not just try to cope with hell, but be compelled—as with all doctrine—to live differently in light of it."[20]

John 3:16 profusely expresses God's great love for everyone. But this tender verse is set in the context of a solemn reminder: "He who believes in Him is not condemned, but he who does not believe is condemned already because he has not believed in the name of the only begotten Son of God" (Jn. 3:18). Peter made it abundantly clear that faith in Jesus is the only way to be reconciled to God. "Salvation is found in no one else, for there is no other name under heaven given to mankind by which we must be saved" (Ac. 4:12, NIV).

If you visit Yale University you will probably see Jonathan Edwards College, the oldest residential college at Yale. The college is named after Jonathan Edwards, renowned theologian and philosopher, third president of Princeton University, and a key figure in America's First Great Awakening. In Edwards' day as well as ours, there were those who took great offense at the prospect of Jesus being the only door to salvation and eternal life. Edwards' response to their criticism is an important rebuttal we need to hear again. As always, Jonathan Edwards exalted the person and work of Jesus Christ:

> *"If God offers you a Saviour from deserved punishment, and you will not receive him, then surely it is just that you should go without a Saviour. Or is God obliged, because you do not like this Saviour, to provide you another? He has given an infinitely honourable and glorious person, even his only begotten Son, to be a sacrifice for sin, and so provided salvation; and this Saviour is offered to you: now if you refuse to accept him, is God therefore unjust if he does not save you? Is he obliged to save you in a way of your own choosing, because you do not like the way of his choosing? Or will you charge Christ with injustice because he does not become your Saviour, when at the same time you will not have him when he offers himself to you, and beseeches you to accept of him as your Saviour?"* [21]

Edwards was both an evangelist and an apologist, a combination sorely needed today. Christianity by its very nature is evangelistic. We are on a rescue mission with eternal consequences. We cannot hope to sustain healthy evangelism and missions if we forfeit the doctrine of eternal judgment for those apart from Christ. This is tantamount to carrying a great cause on a weak foundation. Eventually the cause will topple because of wobbly underpinnings. We must recover a robust, biblical soteriology (doctrine of salvation). In my opinion, no theological issue could be more crucial than how deeply we really believe that people without Christ are eternally lost and that there is salvation in no one else but Jesus Christ. As Calvin Miller wrote, "All universalisms, no matter how reasonable, are hostile to the Great Commission."[22]

Here are some reasons why we must make a forceful response to universalism:

- *It dishonors the cross and the gospel.* To confer an "anonymous Christian" status on those who openly deny Christ's atoning death and His lordship is patently dishonoring to the suffering of Jesus and the clear demands of the gospel.
- *It disregards the overwhelming evidence of Scripture.* Jesus taught that the unbelieving person is "condemned already" and that "the wrath of God abides on him" (John 3:18, 36). Paul made an airtight case for the lostness of humanity in the first chapters of Romans. According to the apostle, even the remotest of peoples are "without excuse" because of the light of conscience and nature. Yet only "the light of the gospel of the glory of Christ" can bring them salvation (2 Cor. 4:4).
- *It diminishes God's holy wrath against sin.* God's character is not on trial. Somewhere deep in our hearts we intuitively know there must be a day of reckoning with a loving, holy God. Universalism denies man freedom of choice. If we remove personal accountability for our actions we deny both the character of God and an essential part of human personality.
- *It dismantles the historic teaching of the church.* To the testimony of the Scriptures and countless Christian martyrs, the historic creeds of the church add their affirmation of a real heaven and a real hell. Most denominations' statements of faith include a clear rejection of universalism. Historically evangelicals have rejected universalism simply because it doesn't line up with the biblical revelation. It is based far more on deductive reasoning than the clear teaching of Scripture.
- *It dilutes the uniqueness of the Christian message.* The uniqueness of Jesus is at the very core of our message and mission. Who is Jesus and what will you do with Him? This is the Great Divide. Under universalism, any road sincerely taken will get you to heaven. But Jesus taught that He was the only way to enter into eternal life and a relationship with God.
- *It deadens the urgency of evangelism.* Urgency is lost because universalism assumes that people either don't need to be saved

or will eventually end up saved. In contrast we believe the gospel is good news only if it arrives in time. But for the universalist the gospel can arrive any time, if indeed it needs to arrive at all. Let's not kid ourselves. If evangelism dies thousands of churches will die too.

- *It dulls the imperative of missions.* One of the clearest injunctions against universalism is the Great Commission itself. Jesus explicitly mandated that we proclaim the gospel to every person and then warned that those who do not believe "will be condemned" (Mk. 16:15-16). Missions rests on several givens, assumptions on which our passion for the Great Commission is built. One of the most basic of these assumptions is that people without Jesus Christ are lost and headed for eternity minus God and minus hope.

Of course, the greatest threat of universalism is to the person outside of Christ. Universalists argue that those who have not responded to the gospel are nonetheless "implicit Christians." They even suggest this should actually increase our motivation for missions! But as John Piper writes, this just doesn't ring true. "On the contrary," Piper responds, "common sense presses another truth on us: the more likely it is that people can be saved without missions the less urgency there is for missions."[23]

The late Roy Fish rhetorically asked, "What does a non-Christian gain by becoming a Christian? Nothing, it seems, that he didn't have before. But shall we then discount the testimony of Hindu or Muslim converts that their conversion was a literal passage from death to life?"[24] We go with the gospel, with all the built-in hazards, precisely because Jesus commands us to go. And He tells us to go because those who die without Him are eternally lost.

WHAT IF THEY HAVEN'T HEARD?

"The elephant in the room" must also be addressed, the issue of those who have never heard the gospel. A young person once came to me with a troubled look on his face. "I believe the Bible," he told me. "But I just can't believe a loving God would condemn someone who has never heard about Jesus." This raises a difficult question. What happens to those who have never heard the gospel?

In the first chapter of Romans, Paul makes a strong case for the lostness of all humanity outside of Jesus Christ. The apostle reminds us that men and women are not only going to be lost when they die; they are born in sin as descendants of Adam and inherently separated from God. Every person stands accountable to God because of the light of conscience and the testimony of God in creation.

The testimony of nature is sometimes called "general revelation." Creation's general revelation of God powerfully preaches our accountability to our Creator. However, only the specific revelation of God in Jesus Christ shows how we can stand justified before Him. It is important to understand that rejection of the gospel is not the only criterion for lostness. Humanity is already lost because of sin. "For all have sinned and fall short of the glory of God" (Ro. 3:23). We are sinners because of the wrongs we have done. We are also sinners because of who we are—children of Adam.

Yet God has gone to the very limits of boundless love to prevent humankind from perishing. The cross of Christ is the roadblock thrown down by a loving God as we raced toward eternal ruin. God incarnate intervened and became sin incarnate on the cross. "He is the atoning sacrifice for our sins, and not only for ours but also for the sins of the whole world" (1 Jn. 2:2). This is the astounding good news of the gospel.

A modified universalist view suggests that only those who

have heard the gospel are accountable. But let's follow that thinking to its logical conclusion. If those who haven't heard are not accountable, we should immediately rush every missionary home and stop every national pastor from reaching any farther. After all, what if those previously unaccountable were to hear the gospel and reject it? They would then be accountable. The missionary would have done them a terrible disservice. Such reasoning would have to conclude that the kindest thing we could do for yet unreached humanity would be to stop proclaiming the gospel! It is little wonder such thinking dwarfs evangelistic outreaches.

The sobering truth is that humanity is accountable to God for their sin. They are headed toward everlasting loss without a saving knowledge of Jesus Christ. David Platt urges us, "We have the gospel of Christ in us, and we do not have time to waste. Some wonder if it is unfair for God to allow so many to have no knowledge of the gospel. But there is no injustice in God. The injustice lies in Christians who possess the gospel and refuse to give their lives to making it known among those who haven't heard."[25]

What a serious accounting awaits us if we believe in eternal judgment for those without faith in Christ—and yet do nothing. I would not want to stand before the Lord as a confessing universalist or a complacent evangelical. Larry Stockstill calls us to a higher vision: "If there are indeed billions of unsaved individuals destined for eternal separation from God, our lives become bigger and more significant than utility bills and relational problems."[26] Let's not just reject faulty theology. Let's embrace those who need Jesus.

TRUTH'S DURABILITY

No matter how upside down many of today's dominant views may be, truth is still truth and falsehoods are still lies. As G. K. Chesterton noted, "Fallacies do not cease to be fallacies because they become fashions."[27]

Those who "get" this gospel message brim over with hope in a world where hope is in critically short supply. The gospel *welcomes* us to read the end of the story first. Yes, there is a great cosmic battle raging this very moment between good and evil. But this is a fixed fight! Victory was assured by Christ's crucifixion and resurrection. Then He broke through all principalities and powers to be seated in highest honor. Jesus "has gone into heaven and is at the right hand of God, angels and authorities and powers having been made subject to Him" (1 Pet. 3:22).

Apologist Nancy Pearcey reminds us, "Christianity is not merely religious truth, it is total truth—truth about the whole of reality."[28] Truth is the most durable of all commodities. That is why the gospel ultimately wins over all distortions, distractions, and assaults. Truth outlasts falsehoods. Truth outlasts its critics. Quoting Chesterton again, "At least five times the Faith has to all appearances gone to the dogs. In each of the five cases, it was the dog that died."[29]

God's love and truth will prevail. "Such is the truth and power of the gospel that the church can be revived, reformed and restored to be a renewing power in the world again," writes Os Guinness.[30] At the end of the day, the church will win. God's kingdom will win. Truth will win. The gospel will triumph. We can rejoice, "having been born again, not of corruptible seed but incorruptible, through the word of God which lives and abides forever. . . . Now this is the word which by the gospel was preached to you" (1 Pet. 1:23, 25).

> Truth is the most durable of all commodities.

SEVEN

THE GOSPEL—

COMMISSIONED FOR ITS ADVANCE

Go into all the world and preach the gospel to all creation.
Mark 16:15, HCSB

The hope of the world rests on the mission of the church; the mission of the church rests on individuals infusing their lives with evangelistic intent.

James Emery White
Serious Times

Our job is to get the gospel to everyone everywhere.

We may start with the friend next door, the person whose desk is next to ours, or perhaps a family member under the same roof. Every breathing human needs Jesus. "I have a great sense of obligation to people in both the civilized world and the rest of the world," Paul wrote, "to the educated and uneducated alike. So I am eager to come to you in Rome, too, to preach the Good News" (Ro. 1:14-15, NLT).

Just as there is only one gospel, there is only one commission. Evangelism (bringing people to Christ) and discipleship (growing believers in Christ) are two parts of a single mandate. Jesus issued what we term the Great Commission in some form in each of the Gospels and also in the Book of Acts. Each time there is an attending promise of supernatural power. In Matthew 28:18-19 before Jesus said, "Go therefore and make disciples of all nations,"

He affirmed, "All authority is given to Me." In Mark 16:15 Jesus commanded His disciples to preach the gospel to every person. Then He promised that signs confirming the gospel will attend those who believe. In Luke 24 He told His disciples they would be witnesses of the things they had seen. But first they must "tarry in the city of Jerusalem until you are endued with power from on high" (v. 49). In John 20:21-22 Jesus commissioned His disciples, "As the Father has sent Me, I also send you." Then immediately He breathed on them and said, "Receive the Holy Spirit." In Acts 1:8 Jesus rebuked activism devoid of spiritual power. How motivated the disciples must have been when the resurrected Christ commanded them to evangelize the world! But then He cooled their heels saying in essence, "Go, but not just yet." Before they became His witnesses, they needed to be empowered by His Spirit.

That same supernatural power to bear witness to the gospel is available to us —now. Even as threats against the gospel intensify we can carry the gospel with joyful confidence. This is a prayer God loves to answer because the results always bring glory to His Son: "Now, Lord, look on their threats, and grant to Your servants that with all boldness they may speak Your word, by stretching out Your hand to heal, and that signs and wonders may be done through the name of Your holy Servant, Jesus" (Ac. 4:29-30). In response, just as He filled those early disciples, He will fill us with His Spirit so we too can proclaim God's good news with boldness.

One day the Great Commission will be the Great Completion. Everything will find its fulfillment in Jesus Christ. "Of the increase of His rule there will be no end!" (Isa. 9:7). There will be new-born people from "all nations, tribes, peoples, and tongues, standing before the throne and before the Lamb" (Rev. 7:9).

Between now and then we are God's delegated witnesses to reach every person on Earth with His message. "Have you thought about his handling of the gospel?" asks John Eldredge.

"God needs to get a message out to the human race, without which they will perish... forever. What's the plan? First, he starts with the most unlikely group ever: a couple of prostitutes, a few fishermen with no better than a second-grade education, a tax collector. Then, he passes the ball to us. Unbelievable."[1]

Yes, and an unbelievable privilege. I'm forever grateful that my life has been drenched in the gospel. From my earliest memories Jesus was center stage. In fact, my mother told me that the first song I went around the house singing was this one: *Send the light, the blessed gospel light!*[2]

Recently my son Jonathan, who serves as president of Global Advance, showed gospel readiness and, in his words, "jumped out of the fishbowl" to minister the love of Christ. Jonathan recounts what happened:

"Today I went to grab my typical fifteen minute lunch. In line I noticed a Hispanic gentleman next to me. Having traveled a lot to Latin countries I decided to practice a little "Espanol con mi hermano." He smiled at my attempts. At the register I said to him, "God bless you" in Spanish.

"He then asked if I was a Christian and I happily replied yes. After I paid for my sandwich I noticed he was seated alone, so I did something unusual. I asked if I could join him for lunch. He seemed a bit surprised but very happy to accommodate. I asked him (Antonio) about his family and job. He shared his story that he came to Texas from Guadalajara when he was 19. He's now 70. He became the head groundskeeper for a wealthy family in our community for over thirty years. It was clear that Antonio was a skilled workman that could be trusted. All four of his children became highly successful. One of them graduated with high honors from Southern Methodist University.

"Antonio shared that the greatest thing that happened to him was finding a relationship with God, something he didn't have at the beginning of his journey. He shared how God miraculously healed

his wife from cancer. He was so happy that all of his children and grandchildren still gather regularly for family time and prayer. Prayer is an important part of their lives, remembering God's grace toward their mother and grandmother.

"At the end of our lunch I prayed with Antonio. I told him his story reminded me how God sent Abraham to another country and blessed his posterity. Antonio replied, 'You didn't just make my day, you made my week!'

"How cool was that! God taught me a great lesson about getting out of my fishbowl. There's an ocean of people all around me from different backgrounds and cultures, people God loves dearly. So I'm challenging my friends and myself to jump out of the fishbowl! God might just surprise you by those you meet."[3]

As I shared earlier the gospel changed everything for our family. It was, is, and forever will be where we drop anchor. Tim Keller writes, "The gospel of grace in Jesus Christ changes everything from our hearts to our community to the world. It completely changes the content, tone, and strategy of all that we do. . . . Because the gospel is endlessly rich, it can handle the burden of being the one 'main thing' of the church."[4]

I'm calling us to once again make the gospel the one main thing in our individual lives and in our churches. As stated in the famous phrase from the Lausanne Covenant, it's time for "the whole church to take the whole gospel to the whole world."[5] I sincerely hope I haven't inferred that gospel proclamation is for preachers only. *Every believer* in Jesus Christ is charged with this commission. *Every believer* is both privileged and obligated to tell this greatest of all stories. Some God-anointed communicators are gifted as evangelists. But *all believers* are entrusted as gospel carriers. The advance of the Christian message has always been primarily through ordinary people who tapped into an extraordinary message. As Michael Green has written, "Christianity was supremely a lay movement, spread by informal missionaries . . . the spontaneous outreach of the total Christian community gave immense impetus to the movement from the very outset."[6]

By All Means, In All Circumstances

Every believer is to share the gospel by every legitimate means. The story is told that Charles Spurgeon was testing the acoustics at the expansive Agricultural Hall in London. Spurgeon was noted for his powerful voice. It was said he could preach to 20,000 and be heard clearly. This was, of course, before the days of sound systems and amplification. In that great hall Spurgeon bellowed out, "Behold the Lamb of God, which taketh away the sin of the world!"

Years later a man approached Spurgeon to thank him. He said that day when Spurgeon had visited the Agricultural Hall he was working in the rafters. Just hearing the preacher quote that great passage from John 1:29 brought him to repentance and faith in Jesus Christ.

This story reminds us that by all means, in all circumstances we should share the gospel. At the turn of this millennium the Billy Graham Evangelistic Association invited thousands of preaching evangelists to Amsterdam. I was privileged to attend this great event. Its purpose was to stimulate world evangelization. At the end of our time together we as delegates affirmed *The Amsterdam Declaration*. This document is now seen as a charter for evangelism in the twenty-first century. It includes this statement: "The records of evangelism from the apostolic age, the state of the world around us today, and the knowledge of Satan's opposition at all times to the spread of the gospel, combine to assure us that evangelistic outreach in the twenty-first century will be an advance in the midst of opposition."[7]

To stand with the gospel is at the same time dangerous and

safe. There is danger because siding with the gospel incurs the wrath of its enemies. There is safety because truth is always a safe (and adventurous) place. Risk is just part of the package of life. If we live large for Jesus our days may see conflict but our sleep will be sweet.

We must be both bold and winsome. Courtesy and courage were displayed in the friendship evangelist George Whitefield cultivated with Benjamin Franklin. Though Franklin had respect for the Christian faith, no evidence suggests he ever made a personal profession of faith in Christ. However, this didn't keep Whitefield from sharing the gospel with him and always keeping communication lines open. Note the gracious yet strong witness of this letter:

London, August 17, 1752

Dear Mr. F--,

*I find that you grow more and more famous in the learned world. As you have made a pretty considerable progress in the mysteries of electricity, I would now humbly recommend to your diligent unprejudiced pursuit and study the mystery of the new birth. It is a most important, interesting study, and when mastered, will richly repay you for all your pains. One, at whose bar we are shortly to appear, hath solemnly declared, that, without it, 'we cannot enter into the kingdom of heaven.' You will excuse this freedom. I must have **aliquid Christi** [something of Christ] in all my letters.*[8]

If Whitefield were alive today no doubt there would be something of Christ in each of his conversations, posts, e-mails, texts, and tweets! We too need to be constantly telling of Jesus. Opportunities are everywhere. May we have eyes to see and wills to quickly take action on the gospel's behalf.

We're to share God's love-message whatever the circumstances and whatever the cost. This is the cause worth living for and dying for. The urgency of our times mandates that we be willing to suffer for the gospel of Christ to be advanced. I call on us this very day to cooperate with the Holy Spirit, allowing Him to prepare us for whatever comes. Our overarching assignment is a yet unfulfilled commission from Jesus.

Being a gospel advocate has never been easy. From the beginning of the church followers of Jesus faced threats, persecution, and often martyrdom. Bishop Stephen Neill reminded his readers of the cost of confessing Christ in the church's infancy. "Every Christian knew that sooner or later he might have to testify to his faith at the cost of his life."[9]

Today the situation is similar in many respects to that faced by the early disciples of Jesus. Like them, we must be adaptable without compromising and gracious in our speech. Like the first century church, today's global church is again becoming a church of miracles, martyrdom, and massive growth.

As did our predecessors, we're to live out the gospel in truth and love. Missionary great Hudson Taylor admonished, "Let them see that you are rejoicing in God, you do not need any other protection, you put your trust in God, you are prepared either to suffer or be delivered as He sees best. They will learn that there is something in the gospel worth risking life for."[10]

More than ever in my lifetime I'm taking special note when I read words like these: "Therefore do not be ashamed of the testimony of our Lord, nor of me His prisoner, but share with me in the sufferings for the gospel according to the power of God" (2 Tim. 1:8). When we're mistreated for Jesus' sake our testimony is only strengthened when we forgive the assailants. Tish Harrison Ward, a campus worker with InterVarsity Christian Fellowship, notes, "We have to forgive and look squarely at those places in our heart that require repentance. In community, we must develop the craft of being both bold and irenic, truthful and humble. And while we grieve rejection, we should not be shocked or ashamed

Playing it safe isn't safe. by it.... From its earliest days, the gospel has been both a comfort and an offense."[11]

Jesus said, "Because iniquity will abound, the love of many will grow cold. But he who endures to the end shall be saved. And this gospel of the kingdom will be preached in all the world as a witness to all nations, and then the end will come" (Matt. 24:12-14). He warned that the love impulse of many would be choked off because of sin and lawlessness. In other words, there is a natural tendency to "circle the wagons" and give our focus and energy to self-preservation. Tragically, many Christians today are in no mood to do anything redemptive for the rest of the world. Yet Jesus prophesied that in the midst of a climate of global anger and recrimination the gospel would go to every nation and people. If we are to respond to the crisis of our times in a God-glorifying way we must recommit ourselves to fulfilling the Great Commission.

"But realize this," Paul counseled, "difficult days will come" (2 Tim. 3:1, NASB). In a real sense these are both the best and worst of times. We cannot be reticent in our gospel witness. Playing it safe isn't safe. Jesus taught that those who are self-protective are actually the most at risk. "Whoever desires to save his life will lose it, but whoever loses His life for My sake and the gospel's will save it" (Mk. 8:34-35).

WHAT ARE WE *FOR*?

Deserved or not, there's a perception among many that evangelical Christians are constantly combative and adversarial. Many know what Bible-believing Christians are against. To stand with the gospel will require that we stand against unscriptural and sometimes anti-scriptural views. Yet in the end our legacy won't be in what falsehoods we denounced but in what truths we upheld. It may surprise some non-Christians to know what principles we advocate.

For starters, Christians have been at the forefront of advocacy for human rights. The most basic of all human rights is the right to hear the gospel and freely respond to it either positively or negatively without fear of reprisal. Frankly, it is the predominance of the gospel within a culture that provides the framework for freedoms enjoyed by all religions. Christians hold firmly to the freedom of any person to worship according to the dictates of his or her conscience.

We also believe in the free exchange of ideas and liberty to share the good news of Jesus Christ with everyone. The gospel is received as the joyful good news by some. Others are offended by it. But as Albert Mohler notes, "The risk of being offended is simply part of what it means to live in a diverse culture that honors and celebrates free speech. A right to free speech means a right to offend; otherwise the right would need no protection."[12]

The Christian faith is set in dazzling juxtaposition to religious dogmas that incite intolerance and violence. Yet some beneficiaries of the very liberty the gospel produces now wish to silence its source. The erosion of biblical values and their benefits calls for today's followers of Jesus to be potent salt and brilliant light.

We believe in freedom of speech, freedom of religion, and freedom of conscience. It is little wonder then that some wish to eradicate the gospel from the public square. Let's not play into their hands by our own silence. We dearly cherish the following freedoms and believe they should be the birthright of every person worldwide:

> The most basic of all human rights is the right to hear the gospel and freely respond to it either positively or negatively without fear of reprisal.

...it is the predominance of the gospel within a culture that provides the framework for freedoms enjoyed by all religions.

Respect for all people. As *The Amsterdam Declaration* affirms, in preaching the gospel "we must do so with love and humility, shunning all arrogance, hostility and disrespect... because all persons are made in the image of God, we must advocate religious liberty and human rights for all. We pledge ourselves to treat those of other religions with respect and faithfully and humbly serve the nation in which God has placed us, while affirming that Christ is the one and only Savior of the world."[13]

Biblical tolerance that grants each person the right to worship according to the dictates of his conscience. We recognize that only the Holy Spirit can convict people of their need of Christ and only He does the work of regeneration. What passes today for tolerance is often merely a lack of conviction. Tolerance is a virtue only if a person believes something strongly and yet respects the right of others to disagree. While I am completely convinced that Jesus is the sole hope of salvation, this does not give me *carte blanche* to be discourteous to others. On the contrary, my total confidence in the gospel frees me to interact with courtesy and respect toward all people, no matter what they believe. We recognize the gospel has both glory and "bite" in its message. Some people will be offended by its affirmations. Resistance to the gospel should fortify our witness all the more. "We were bold in our God to speak to you the gospel of God in much conflict" (1 Thess. 2:2).

The right to proclaim the gospel and evangelize unbelievers. Anti-conversion laws are springing up in many countries as hostility to Christians mounts. Ours is the position of *The Millennial Manifesto* crafted by the AD 2000 and Beyond Movement:

"We reject all forms of coercive proselytism and manipulative pressure, but uphold the right of persons to become followers of Jesus in response to the conviction of the Holy Spirit."[14]

Speaking the truth in love, as the Bible tells us to do, is not hate speech. It is mandated in Scripture, motivated by love, and part of what it means to have freedom of speech. Nor should earnest appeals, born out of love and concern, be considered manipulative. No one, no matter what his faith, should ever be prevented from urging others to embrace a conviction he firmly believes. Vishal and Ruth Mangalwadi remind us, "Freedom of conscience is incomplete without the freedom to change one's beliefs, to convert. A state that hinders conversion is uncivilized because it restricts the human quest for truth and reform."[15]

Whether we speak freely or under threats, still we must speak. "For we cannot but speak the things which we have seen and heard" (Ac. 4:20). The most benevolent activity possible—the activity that undergirds all other ministry—is evangelism, telling the good news of salvation through Jesus Christ.

URGENT AND COMPASSIONATE

Thom Ranier, a skilled observer of church trends and president and CEO of Lifeway Christian Resources, recently listed fifteen reasons why churches today are less evangelistic than in the past. Topping the list: "Christians have no sense of urgency to reach lost people."[16] Today we must recover a biblically-based sense of urgency, and here's why.

Our opportunities have a limited shelf life. Every day of freedom to share the gospel in today's world is a great gift. With the potential of disruptive terrorism escalating rapidly we should pray with the Psalmist, "Teach us to number our days" (Psa. 90:12). Someone has observed that the opportunity of a lifetime must be seized within the lifetime of the opportunity. There are colossal doors of opportunity wide open for the gospel in many parts of the world, and they may not be open long.

Life itself is short. James calls it "a vapor that appears for a little time and then vanishes" (Jas. 4:14). Certainly there is an urgency for those who do not know Jesus Christ. But are we conveying this to them? Deitrich Bonhoeffer wrote, "Nothing could be more ruthless than to make men think there is still plenty of time to mend their ways. To tell men that the cause is urgent, and that the kingdom of God is at hand is the most charitable and merciful act we can perform, the most joyous news we can bring."[17]

The season of harvest is brief. I was raised in the city. I don't know much about farming. But I do know this much: when it's harvest time there's nothing else on the agenda. The one and only priority is to get the harvest safely in.

Harvest by its very nature is not open-ended; there is a *season* of harvest. One of the saddest verses in the Bible is Jeremiah 8:20, "The harvest is past, the summer is ended, and we are not saved." Jesus warned us not to look for a more opportune time but to put in the sickle now. "Lift up your eyes, and see that the fields are white for harvest" (Jn. 4:35). There is a vast, ripe spiritual harvest worldwide right now—and it is threatened because we aren't reaping it! God give us leaders who feel the urgency of our task and can transmit that urgency to others.

Eternity is long. Our urgency is theologically based. The intensity of our urgency will be in direct proportion to how much we genuinely believe people without Christ are truly lost. To use the old term, they are literally *unsaved*. There's a clear correlation: the church's evangelistic passion has waned as its belief in eternal judgment has weakened.

The gospel is the power of God for salvation—not for everyone automatically—but for all who believe on the Lord Jesus Christ (Ro. 1:16; 10:9). But the gospel must be *proclaimed* in order to be believed. "How can they call on him to save them unless they believe in him? And how can they believe in him if they have never heard about him? And how can they hear about him unless someone tells them?" (Ro. 10:14, NLT).

The story of Cornelius dramatically illustrates this. Cornelius was devout, prayed often, was well respected, gave generously to the poor, and even had an angelic visitation. Pretty strong credentials. Yet God went to great lengths to get the gospel to him so he could come to faith in Christ and be saved! The biblical account clearly shows that Peter did not consider Cornelius forgiven of his sins until he believed the message of the gospel. In fact, the angel instructed Cornelius to send for Peter "who will tell you words by which you and all your household will be saved" [future tense] (Ac. 11:14). The good works of religious Cornelius did not and could not save him. He had to hear and then believe the gospel.

All the gospel "invitations" in the New Testament are in the imperative mood. The gospel is not a choice to consider, it is a command either to obey or reject. You can forestall an invitation with nebulous niceties. But you must either obey or reject a command. The gospel doesn't merely invite belief. It demands it. "Repent, and believe the gospel" (Mk. 1:15).

Christianity by its very nature is evangelistic. Evangelism is based on the assumption, massively supported by Scripture, that people who are without Jesus Christ are lost. We are on a rescue mission with eternal consequences. If people are lost without Christ (and they are), and if faith in Christ is the only avenue of salvation (and it is), what could possibly be a higher priority than getting the gospel as far as we can as fast as we can?

Compassionate urgency makes all the difference. In the formative days of the ministry of The Navigators, its founder, Dawson Trotman, was heartbroken by what he saw on an overseas trip. Many people were engaged in religious practices with no hope of forgiveness and cleansing. Trotman wrote back to his young Navigators, "Kids, we've got the truth to dispel this darkness. We've got to get it out, out, OUT!"[18] That's the kind of passion and urgency that births, and sustains, world-class churches and ministries.

All this promoting of evangelism may lead some to ask, "But what about discipleship? Isn't discipleship even more important than evangelism?" The answer is no, because without evangelism there would be no believers to disciple. I agree that disciple-making is extremely important and should always accompany evangelism. As stated earlier, evangelism and discipleship are two sides of the same coin. *Preach the gospel / make disciples*— that's the essence of the Great Commission. Evangelism will always accompany true discipleship. The core of discipleship is following Jesus. And Jesus said that when we follow Him we will share the gospel with others. "Follow Me, and I will make you fishers of men" (Matt. 4:19). There is no such thing as non-evangelistic discipleship.

We are *witnesses* to the power of the gospel (Ac. 1:8, Ro. 1:16). We are *ministers* of reconciliation (2 Cor. 5:18). We are *ambassadors* for Christ (2 Cor. 5:20). When we truly grasp this we will never again wonder about our destiny. A holy imperative will impel us: "Woe is me if I do not preach the gospel!" (1 Cor. 9:16). We're under mandate. So we carry the gospel with urgency, compassion, sensitivity to people, sensitivity to the Holy Spirit, authority, and confidence. What a calling; what an honor! We represent Jesus Christ and His gospel in our time.

> For the church to go forward in this hour we must go back— back to the centrality of the gospel.

The gospel is to be shared by all believers, including children. It is by no means the property of preachers only. In fact, often the most effective witness is outside the walls of the church. Christian business persons speak of "the 9 to 5 Window" of ministry opportunities at the workplace.

For the church to go forward in this hour we must go back—back to the centrality of the gospel. We have wearied ourselves in any number of good causes while putting the gospel itself on the back burner. Starting now, let's once again make the main thing the main thing. The church must return to compassionate, Christ-centered evangelism as its primary activity. Theologian Carl F. H. Henry reminded us, "The gospel is good news only if it arrives in time."[19] God, make us urgent. And may the gospel arrive in time.

THE NEED FOR APOLOGETICS

Peter says we are to "always be prepared to give an answer to everyone who asks you to give the reason for the hope that you have, but do this with gentleness and respect" (1 Pet. 3:15, NIV). The thought in the original language carries the directive, "Be ready to give a defense." The word translated *defense* or *answer* is the Greek word *apologia*. It's the same word Paul used in Philippians 1:17 when he declared, "I am appointed for the defense of the gospel." From this Greek word we derive the word *apologetics*, a rational defense of our faith. Far from inferring that we're in any way embarrassed or "apologetic" about the gospel, the ministry of apologetics actually prevents any awkward shyness regarding the gospel's veracity.

A special bond forms among those who stand in solidarity together for the faith. Paul said fellow defenders of the faith were "in my heart . . . and in the defense and confirmation of the gospel, you all are partakers with me of grace" (Phil. 1:7). A strong part of our stewardship as those entrusted with the gospel is to protect its truth. When anyone messed with the gospel Paul sprang into action. "We did not give in to them for a moment, so that the truth of God might be preserved for you" (Gal. 2:5, NIV).

Apologetics has enormous value not only for skeptics and also for committed followers of Christ. Nancy Pearcey observes, "Today basic apologetics has become a crucial skill for sheer survival. Without the tool of apologetics, young people can be solidly trained in Bible study and doctrine, yet still flounder helplessly when they leave home and face the secular world on their own."[20]

The ministry of apologetics also greatly benefits non-Christians. My longtime friend, Jim Burkett, notes, "Apologetics clears the way for evangelism. It removes the intellectual obstacles and identifies the false concepts that have prevented a person from understanding Christ and the gospel. Apologetics leads a person to the reasonableness of Christianity and to the place where he can hear the gospel of Christ and make a choice."[21]

God greatly used John Stott as a brilliant apologist, theologian, and evangelist. May his prayer be ours, as well: "I pray earnestly that God will raise up today a new generation of Christian apologists or Christian communicators, who will combine an absolute loyalty to the biblical gospel and an unwavering confidence in the power of the Spirit with a deep and sensitive understanding of the contemporary alternatives to the gospel, who will relate the one to the other with freshness, pungency, authority and relevance; and who will use their minds to reach other minds for Christ."[22]

THE DIFFERENCE YOU MAKE

Still, for many there seems to be a dark canopy over the truth of the gospel. They just don't get it; they just can't see it. Paul addressed this when he noted, "But even if our gospel is veiled, it is veiled to those who are perishing, whose minds the god of this age has blinded, who do not believe, lest the light of the gospel of the glory of Christ, who is the image of God, should shine on them" (2 Cor. 4:2-4).

Evangelism then involves not only the convincing of the mind but also the unshackling of the will. It is a spiritual eye surgery on those who have been blinded by unbelief. That is why intercessory prayer is so crucial to our gospel efforts. Before we talk to people about God we should talk to God about people. Through prayer we wrench people out from the hold of the enemy, freeing their minds and wills to accept the gospel message.

Antecedent to any great move of God, somebody somewhere has been weeping instead of sleeping, agonizing before God for those who have not yet come to Jesus. Many years ago I read a tract entitled, "How I Learned to Pray for the Lost." In this tract the author said, "I have taken my place of authority in Christ and am using it against the enemy. I have not looked to myself to see if I am fit or not; I have just taken my place and prayed that the Holy Spirit may do His convicting work. If each and every member of the Body of Christ would do this, what a change would be made in this world."[23]

God has woven the principle of cause and effect into the system of His creation. Things happen because of some previous action. This is certainly true regarding our prayers that those who haven't yet done so will place their faith in Christ. Dick Eastman writes, "I am convinced that when we stand before God . . . we will discover that every soul ever brought to a knowledge of Christ was in some way related to intercessory prayer."[24] *Your prayers make a world of difference.*

Also, *your verbal witness makes a world of difference.* When we pray for the lost we also need to pray for ourselves, that we will be sensitive to the Spirit's promptings and boldly share the good news of Jesus. "Pray also for me," Paul requested, "that whenever I speak, words may be given to me so that I will fearlessly make known the mystery of the gospel" (Eph. 6:19, NIV).

Who can know what leading just one child to Jesus might set in motion?

"A Sunday school teacher in Boston took a Saturday to visit each boy in his class. He wanted to be sure they had all come to know Christ. One boy worked as a clerk in his uncle's shoe store. Edward Kimball entered the store, walked back to the stockroom where Dwight Lyman Moody was stocking the shelves, and confronted the youth with the importance of knowing Christ personally. In that stockroom D.L. Moody accepted Christ as his Savior. Kimball had no idea that this act of faithfulness on his part would reap such a rich harvest for heaven. It has been estimated that during his lifetime D.L. Moody traveled more than a million miles and spoke to more than 100 million people.

"It was D.L. Moody who led Wilbur Chapman to the Lord. Chapman became a great evangelist in the generation succeeding Moody's. During Chapman's ministry in Chicago, a baseball player with the White Stockings had a Sunday off and was standing in front of a bar on State Street in Chicago. A gospel team from the Pacific Garden Mission came by, playing hymns and inviting people to the afternoon service down the street. The ballplayer, recognizing the hymns of his childhood, attended the service and received Christ as his personal Savior.

"That afternoon encounter with Christ dramatically changed the life of Billy Sunday. He played ball several more years and then Chapman invited Billy Sunday to join his crusade team as an advance man, to help organize pastors and set up the evangelistic meetings. Sunday enthusiastically agreed. Two years later, Chapman left the evangelistic ministry to become the pastor of one of the leading churches in America. Sunday felt stranded, but he refocused on national crusade evangelism and soon began to schedule his own crusades.

"During Billy Sunday's meetings in Charlotte, North Carolina, Sunday encouraged the formation of a Christian Men's Club to promote evangelism in the city. A few years later the Charlotte Christian Men's Club invited Mordecai Ham to hold evangelistic meetings in Charlotte. As was usual in Ham's meetings, massive

crowds came to hear him preach. In one of those large crowds one night, a young man named Billy Graham came forward to accept Christ."

"What a phenomenal succession of faithful and stellar harvesters for the cause of eternity," notes Joseph Stowell. "Edward Kimball was simply an unheralded follower who gave up a Saturday for the cause. Heaven is crowded with the results of his routine faithfulness."[25]

This "golden chain of evangelism" began with a little-known man, Edward Kimball. In heaven, before I meet the gospel luminaries who came to Christ through the reverberations of his witness, I want to meet Mr. Kimball. When you get to heaven will there be anyone waiting to meet you? Will anyone say to you, "I'm here because of your witness. You kept holding on when I was holding out. Thank you for sharing the gospel with me"? That, indeed, will be a crown of rejoicing. "For what is our hope, or joy, or crown of rejoicing? Is it not even you in the presence of our Lord Jesus Christ at His coming?" (1 Thess. 2:19).

THE HOPE OF THE GOSPEL

I took a good look at Javier's feet. Along with another Tsetsil Indian pastor, Javier had trekked three days through the mountains of Chiapas, Mexico, to be equipped for more effective outreach. Like most of the Majority World pastors Global Advance is privileged to serve, Javier had no formal training for ministry. Having heard there was ministry training in his area, he thought it was worth a three-day walk.

I watched Pastor Javier throughout the conference. Sometimes he would just drink in the teaching with a big smile. At other times, he was feverishly taking notes. Sometimes, he would just silently weep as God's Spirit ministered to him. Now at the end of the conference he came up to me to say thanks. He did not speak English or Spanish. I didn't speak his Tsetsil dialect. So he thanked me for the training in a more profound way. He just put his head on my chest and cried.

As I embraced this precious brother I looked again at his feet. They were still swollen from his half-week walk over rugged terrain. They were dusty and calloused. Their only protection was a pair of thin moccasins that appeared to be hand-sewn. I looked again and remembered, "How beautiful upon the mountains are the feet of him who brings good news; who proclaims peace, who brings glad tidings, who proclaims salvation" (Isa. 52:7).

I dedicate this final chapter to the beautiful believers carrying this beautiful gospel, propelled by beautiful feet. At least they look that way to God. Javier's feet and the feet of all gospel carriers are protected by battle-tempered footwear. "For shoes, put on the peace that comes from the Good News so that you will be fully prepared" (Eph. 6:15, NLT). Now we are ready to engage the enemy, not with rage and brutality but with the peace only the gospel brings. Curtis Vaughan details this essential piece of the gospel-carrier's uniform:

> "The well-equipped soldier in Paul's day wore sandals with soles thickly studded with hobnails. Such sandals not only gave protection to the feet but also enabled the soldier to move quickly and surely. In ancient times, when warfare was largely a matter of hand-to-hand combat, this quickness of movement was essential. The Christian, Paul explains, must have on his feet 'the preparation of the gospel of peace' (vs. 15). Most interpreters understand 'preparation' in the sense of 'readiness' to serve God. The idea is that of a disposition of mind that makes men quick to see their duty and ever ready to plunge into the fight. This readiness comes from, or is produced by, 'the gospel of peace.' This gospel is so designated because it is a peace-bringing power that destroys the enmity in men's hearts and establishes tranquility in its place (cf. Isa. 52:7). It is this

heart-peace produced by the gospel that gives the Christian warrior his readiness for combat. To have a consciousness of peace with God and to live in tranquil communion with Him enables one to fling himself into the battle with strong determination and calm assurance."[26]

Let's join Pastor Javier in paying whatever cost necessary to bring honor to Jesus in our time. "Your name and renown are the desire of our hearts" (Isa. 26:8, NIV). His gospel is for every person, every place, every problem. The gospel is superior to every rival, every principality, every power. As Tim Keller says, "The gospel has supernatural versatility to address the particular hopes, fears, and idols of every culture and every person."[27]

This good news of Jesus Christ is worthy of our all. As Henry Drummond admonished, "If you know anything better, live for it; if not, in the name of God and of Humanity, carry out Christ's plan."[28] May Paul's expectation be ours, as well: "For I fully expect and hope that I will never be ashamed, but that I will continue to be bold in Christ. . . And I trust that my life will bring honor to Christ, whether I live or die" (Phil. 1:20, NLT).

It would be unconscionable to close this chapter without a final appeal to anyone reading who has not yet come to the Savior. I wish you could see me as I write these words. My eyes are moist with tears. I'm praying—for you. I plead with you, come to Jesus. Come now. He promises, "The one who comes to Me I will by no means cast out" (Jn. 6:37). Make this the prayer of your heart:

Lord Jesus, thank You for dying on the cross for me. Right now I repent of my sins and trust Your shed blood as the full payment for all my sins. I believe that You are the Son of God and that God has raised You from the dead. I now receive You as my personal Savior. I commit my life to You as my Lord. You are now in charge of my life. Thank You for hearing my prayer, forgiving my sins, and coming into my life as You promised. Amen."[29]

For every Christian reading, I also plead with you: take the gospel radically. Richard Niebuhr observed, "The great Christian revolutions come not by the discovery of something that was not known before. They happen when somebody takes radically something that was always there."[30] A gospel-anchored life takes the Great Commission radically. Radicals from other religions often destroy; gospel radicals rebuild. Radicals of other faiths are known to put to death the living; gospel radicals bring the spiritually dead to life.

Pastor Robert Morris admonishes us, "Never get over your testimony."[31] Let your personal experience of grace freshly wash over your soul today. In your heart go back to where it all began with Jesus. Never leave your first love (Rev. 2:4). There are days when our stewardship burns with holy passion within us. There may be other days when the heavens seem like brass and we would like to run away. But just keep telling the story. "If I preach voluntarily, I have a reward; if not voluntarily, I am simply discharging the trust committed to me" (1 Cor. 9:17, NIV). Whatever your feelings, *anchor* your life in the gospel.

I must take a cue from Paul, remembering his parting words to the Ephesian elders. He committed them to God and to the word of His grace. Even as the gospel had been entrusted to him, Paul then entrusted the church at Ephesus to God's care and to the gospel's reconstructive power. As Paul assured them, "The word of his grace . . . is able to build you up and give you an inheritance with all those he has set apart for himself" (Ac. 20:32, NLT).

As a redeemed man entrusted with the gospel I now commit this book to God and to the gospel's global advance. I confess I was tempted to run from this assignment. It just seemed too colossal. I was almost frightened, and certainly humbled, by the sheer prospect of my frail words being a printed proponent of the Message above all others. Yet, excluding the human authors of Scripture, how can anyone fully do justice to such a sublime topic as the gospel of Jesus Christ?

I'm sure that as soon as *Entrusted* goes to press I'll think, "Oh, I should have said this...." After all, how could I ever say enough about the gospel? And regarding what I have written, no doubt I will sorely wish I would have or could have said it better. But because of the acute need for this book it's time to stop polishing. Now it's time to publish. So I release this book, confidently imploring God's Spirit to breathe on it, give it life, and give it wings.

George Whitefield described Theodore Frelinghuysen as "a worthy old soldier of Jesus Christ."[32] Whatever our age we should aspire to be worthy soldiers of the cross of Christ. When or if people remember me I hope to be thought of simply as "the brother whose praise is in the gospel" (2 Cor. 8:18).

I'm as passionate to reach people with the gospel as when God first called me to preach. In fact, the flame burns brighter as the years pass. This will always be my most important book. If this old soldier could leave one gift for you it would be the heart-cry I've worked to inject into each sentence. It is Christ's pulsating commission to proclaim the good news to all creation.

When you said yes to Jesus, you became heir to "the hope which is laid up for you in heaven, of which you heard before in the word of the truth of the gospel" (Col. 1:5). Cherish that hope. Prize your stewardship. Exalt Jesus and His atoning work. Make the gospel the center. Guard it as life's greatest treasure. Share it as history's greatest announcement. Preach it to yourself. Proclaim it to the world. You are entrusted with the gospel.

AFTERWORD

This book was written against the backdrop of a pronounced spike in the persecution of Christians around the world. Hymn writer Isaac Watts asked, "Is this vile world a friend to grace, to help me on to God?"[1] The glaring answer—this world is no "friend to grace." It often seems that the vilifying of God's great love-message is almost ubiquitous.

John speaks of "those who had been beheaded for their witness to Jesus and for the word of God" (Rev. 20:4). That no longer sounds like vague eschatology; it sounds more like this morning's grim news. Barbarous acts including crucifixions and beheadings are on the rise. Tens of thousands of Christians have been forced into nomadic exile fleeing radical religious terrorists. Churches have been bombed in cruel plots to intimidate believers from assembly and public worship. Most every Christian senses that the heat of opposition is noticeably hotter than in the past.

Clearly the gospel is perceived as a threat, and it is. It confronts every system, every ideology, indeed, every person who will not bow to Jesus. Yet its message brims with love, hope, and mercy. Such is the majesty of our message. It is revolutionary by its very nature. History has shown the gospel to be the single most transformative pronouncement ever given. Forces belligerent against the gospel intuitively know this. That is why there is such an aggressive global campaign to silence its proclamation or at least marginalize our witness.

History has shown the gospel to be the single most transformative pronouncement ever given.

In the midst of these challenges our commission as gospel carriers has not been rescinded. In fact, our mandate is increasingly urgent. The need for the gospel is greater than ever. The cry of a

...our call is to fully engage in honorably stewarding and furthering the gospel in our time.

sin-battered world for the gospel is stronger than ever. The hope of the gospel shines brighter than ever.

Having anchored our lives to the immovable rock of the gospel, we must now take action on its behalf. Above all I want those who don't know Jesus personally to know Him and experience His pardon and power. For those of us who are His followers, our call is to fully engage in honorably stewarding and furthering the gospel in our time.

Here's a review of some major points and some suggestions on how we can faithfully discharge this priceless stewardship entrusted to us.

Rehearse your gospel benefits. The gospel is the source from which all blessings flow. Every New Testament promise and blessing is embedded in the gospel. Every good gift is because, thanks to the gospel, we are "in Christ" with all the attending benefits that status brings us. Luther encouraged Christians, "Preach the gospel to yourself every day."[2] "He who did not spare His own Son, but gave Him up for us all, how shall He not with Him also freely give us all things?" (Rom. 8:32).

Put in a good word for Jesus. Regrettably, many people so routinely profane Jesus' name in their normal conversation it has become an unconscious habit. Let's counter by honoring Jesus in our everyday speech so much that the intentional becomes habitual. Each day insert Jesus into your conversations. This may not be a full blown gospel presentation but our "good word for Jesus" can act as pre-evangelism, preparing the hearts of hearers. God places some people in our path for us to sow the gospel seed. In others' lives we water seed already sown. Then there are those thrilling encounters when we reap a ripened harvest God has prepared.

Make a beeline for the cross. Spurgeon's exhortation to fellow-preachers desperately needs to be heeded today. He said that, whatever his text, he always made "a beeline for the cross." May it be so with all preachers. The Ethiopian consul chose the text but Philip chose the subject. The evangelist "opened his mouth, and beginning at this Scripture, preached Jesus to him" (Ac. 8:35). Something I so appreciate about Franklin Graham is how, like his father, he "makes a beeline for the cross." Whether he's being interviewed about a humanitarian project or preaching in a large evangelistic meeting the gospel is first and foremost. The gospel is always to be preached "as of first importance" (1 Cor. 15:3, NIV).

Watch for sovereign set-ups. Often God orchestrates who our server will be at a restaurant or who will sit next to us on a plane. Ask the Holy Spirit to sensitize you to the needs of people you interact with every day. So many people are riddled with pain. Their spiritual search floats just below the surface. When they are "touched by a loving heart, wakened by kindness,"[3] the door for gospel witness can fling open.

Create a gospel culture. God's grace rescued me early in life—and I'm eternally grateful. Grateful most of all for Jesus. Grateful for parents who exposed me from my earliest days to the gospel and created a culture of love, grace, and whole-hearted devotion to Christ. Grateful for a strong support system of church, friends, and "missional living" (long before this term was used). Grateful for the dignity and purpose a life promoting the gospel brings. People are watching how we respond to life's wins and losses. When they observe us may they see gospel fallout everywhere, that our lives are truly anchored in the gospel.

Leverage your megaphone. Social media is both a blessing and a bane. Notwithstanding the electronic world's downside, it's amazing that we can have immediate, international impact by words we unleash. Frankly I'm disturbed by the amount of negativity coming from Christians digitally. Let's bring *good news*!

Can you imagine how the apostle Paul might have leveraged such potential? A free but faithful paraphrase of Proverbs 25:11 for today might read, "A word fitly tweeted is like apples of gold in settings of silver." A small gospel injection into digital media can indeed go a long way.

Work at winsomeness. One of the great challenges for Bible-believing Christians in our day is to proclaim and defend truth with civility. The gospel is not served by either a hermit-like retreat from culture or incessantly angry denunciations against it. "No man is an island," wrote preacher-poet John Donne, keying off Romans 14:7. God wants us to fully engage life and that means we engage people and culture. Let's remember and practice Paul's *modus operandi*: "I have become all things to all people, that by all means I might save some. I do it all for the sake of the gospel, that I might share with them in its blessings" (1 Cor. 9:22-23, ESV).

Love your enemies. No matter how gracious we are, also like Paul, we will have enemies. Jesus is clear that we are to love them (Matt. 5:44). Ultimately, people are not the enemy. They are victims of the enemy. Our real adversary is the devil (1 Pet. 5:8). Although some who oppose the gospel may never respond, there are many others who are ready and waiting to be loved into God's kingdom.

Draw on God's resources. The Holy Spirit is ever pointing people to Jesus. He is the great evangelist. We are to cooperate with Him (Rev. 22:17). When invited He will always attend the proclaiming of the gospel. The Holy Spirit prepares hearts for the implanted word that brings salvation. We should expect miraculous signs that attest to the power and veracity of the good news we bring. "For the testimony of Jesus is the spirit of prophecy" (Rev. 19:10). The Word of God energized by the Spirit of God is a formidable, God-ordained combination.

Pray for the success of the gospel. Paul asked friends to pray "that the word of the Lord may run swiftly and be glorified" (2 Thess.

3:1). We're to pray in faith that the spiritual cataracts will fall from unbelievers' eyes, in order that "the light of the gospel of the glory of Christ, who is the image of God, should shine on them" (2 Cor. 4:4). Start a prayer list

...leverage your life for the gospel.

today of those in your sphere of influence who need the Lord Jesus. Pray in faith that they will hear and respond to the gospel. Then stand ready to be God's instrument to see your faith made sight.

Share the gospel no matter what your circumstances. Here again, the apostle Paul serves as a sterling example. He preached the gospel in the shadow of the daunting pagan Parthenon in Athens. He reasoned with the Jews in synagogues from Jerusalem to Rome. He preached freely in marketplaces and sang praises to Jesus at the risk of his life in jail. His legal defenses became the platform for evangelistic sermons. And under the watchful eye of a government-ordered guard, Paul "proclaimed the kingdom of God and taught about the Lord Jesus Christ—with all boldness and without hindrance!" (Ac. 28:31, NIV). Most of Paul's life after his conversion was lived under the pressure of threats from religious and government authorities. This did not deter him from his primary mission: "the ministry which I received from the Lord Jesus, to testify to the gospel of the grace of God" (Ac. 20:24). Whether free, persecuted, or imprisoned the mandate remains: "Go into all the world and preach the gospel to all creation" (Mk. 16:15). Determine that no matter your condition or location you will share the gospel with someone in some way every day.

Look to the reward. Jesus endured the cross "for the joy that was set before Him" (He.12:2). What He saw by faith was that His atoning work would "bring many sons to glory" (He. 2:10). A crown of rejoicing awaits believers who bring others to faith in Christ (1 Thess. 2:19).

This isn't an exhaustive list but it offers some good starting points for our stewardship. The Holy Spirit will reveal more ways you can be an effective gospel carrier. My ardent prayer is that God will use what you have read to stir you to leverage your life for the gospel. If you will come before the Lord with a blank check of your life, allowing Him to write in all the particulars, astounding things will begin to happen.

At the core of who I am, I long to see Jesus intimately known, devotedly loved, radically obeyed, and lavishly worshiped by redeemed people out of every tribe, language, and nation. But this dream has a price.

A few years ago I stood in silent awe viewing the acres of graves of 9387 soldiers buried on the peaceful cliff above Omaha Beach in Normandy, France. This place, now sacred and serene, was the scene of history's largest military invasion which commenced June 6, 1944. My time there was a sobering, profound reminder that real wars exact real casualties. Hugely significant victories require hugely significant sacrifices. Our battle is not against people. It is, however, a hugely significant conflict for the hearts and minds of this generation. The stakes are every bit as high as those faced by the soldiers who hit that beach many decades ago. The casualties are just as real. For us as well, victory will require our all, whether by life or by death.

General Dwight Eisenhower, Supreme Commander of the Allied Forces in Europe, understood that the cost of establishing a beachhead on the European continent would be colossal. Thousands of young lives would be sacrificed, thousands of families' stories forever altered. But Eisenhower also knew that on the day that beachhead was secured victory was no longer just a possibility. Victory was inevitable.

On the day Jesus walked up Calvary's hill the ultimate triumph of the gospel was irrevocably secured. A "kingdom beachhead" has been established that will ultimately blanket the entire earth. Victory is now inevitable. The Father has sworn by His own name that He will bring global glory to His Son. When all the smoke finally clears, every knee will bow to Him (Phil. 2:9-11). As William Carey wrote after he had suffered his greatest setback, "God's cause will triumph."[4]

So lift up your head and "continue in the faith, grounded and steadfast… not moved away from the hope of the gospel" (Col. 1:23). You represent Christ's interests and those of His kingdom in the world. As an emissary of the gospel of Jesus Christ, God's consummate love-message to all creation has been *entrusted— to you*. Now shine the dazzling light of God's redeeming love in every way to everyone everywhere!

Then be at rest. No matter how bleak today may seem God's cause will triumph. Until then—sow in faith, water in hope, speak the truth, live in love. Anchor your life in the gospel.

NOTES

INTRODUCTION

[1] See http://www.christianitytoday.com/ch/asktheexpert/sep13.html. Accessed November 10, 2014.

[2] Johannes Gutenberg (c.1395-c.1468) was a German inventor who developed a method of printing from moveable type. His printing press changed history, launching the quick disseminating of information through print. Gutenberg's 42-line Bible was the first major book printed with moveable type in the West. Fifty years after his death his invention was crucial to the rapid spread of the Reformation through mass publication of tracts and portions of Scripture. In turn, the proliferation of the Bible was strategic to recovering the primacy and purity of the gospel.

[3] This term was first coined in *Soul Searching: The Religious and Spiritual Lives of American Teenagers* (2005) by Christian Smith and Melinda Lundquist Denton.

CHAPTER ONE

[1] Ruth A. Tucker, *Stories of Faith* (Grand Rapids, MI: Zondervan, 1989), 245. Robert J. Morgan, *On This Day* (Nashville, TN: Thomas Nelson, 1997), 6.

[2] http://berean.org/wb.html. Accessed August 21, 2014.

[3] http://www.spurgeon.org/sermons/3278.htm. Accessed June 30, 2014.

[4] Quoted in David Shibley, *Everything I Need to Know I Learned in Sunday School* (Green Forest, AR: New Leaf Press, 1996), 20.

[5] Oswald Chambers, *My Utmost for His Highest* (New York: Dodd, Mead, & Co., 1935), 91.

[6] This aspect of the good news, emphasizing the redemption of all creation, is termed "the gospel in the air" by Matt Chandler in *The Explicit Gospel*. The focus of my book is that aspect of the gospel that spotlights redemption for all people who turn from self and sin and place their faith in Christ. Both components are vital for a full-orbed appreciation of the biblical gospel which culminates in Christ's kingdom and unrivaled rule over all creation.

[7] Rice Broocks, *God's Not Dead* (Nashville, TN: Thomas Nelson, 2013), 16.

[8] Ed Stetzer, "Defining the Gospel: Some Examples from My Class at Wheaton." http://www.christianitytoday.com/edstetzer/2014/july/morning-roundup-72214.html. Accessed July 22, 2014.

[9] Ché Ahn, *Fire Evangelism* (Grand Rapids, MI: Chosen, 2006), 78.

[10] Steve Murrell, *100 Years from Now* (Nashville, TN: Dunham Books, 2013), 7.

[11] "Love Crucified Arose!" by Michael Card is an enduring anthem of contemporary Christian music.

[12] Henry Blackaby, *Experiencing the Cross* (Colorado Springs, CO: Multnomah Books, 2005), 58.

[13] "I Love to Tell the Story" by Catherine Haney. Public domain.

[14] D. Martyn Lloyd-Jones, *Preaching and Preachers* (Grand Rapids, MI:

Zondervan, 1972), 87.

[15]Jared C. Wilson, *Gospel Wakefulness* (Wheaton, IL: Crossway, 2011), 203.

[16]"There Is a Fountain" by William Cowper. Public domain.

Chapter Two

[1]http://www.christianitytoday.com/edstetzer/2015/march/dont-miss-story-of-bible. Accessed March 31, 2015.

[2]"Let Earth and Heaven Combine," by Charles Wesley. Public domain.

[3]"Meekness and Majesty," by Graham Kendrick. © 1986, Kingsway's Thankyou Music, admin. EMI Christian Music Publishing.

[4]F. F. Bruce, "The Person and Work of Christ: Incarnation and Virgin Birth," *Basic Christian Doctrines*, Carl F. H. Henry, ed. (New York: Holt, Rinehart and Winston, 1962), 125.

[5]http://zinzendorf.com/pages/index.php?id=ecce-homo. Accessed July 9, 2014. See also David Shibley, *Great for God* (Green Forest, AR: New Leaf Press, 2012), 122.

[6]Robert E. Speer, *The Finality of Jesus Christ* (Fleming H. Revell, 1933, assigned to Grand Rapids, MI: Zondervan Publishing House, 1968), 232.

[7]Paul E. Little, *Know What You Believe* (Downers Grove, IL: IVP Books, 2003), 61-62. Based on A. H. Strong, *Systematic Theology* (Philadelphia, PA: Judson Press, 1907), 673.

[8]David Platt, *Radical* (Colorado Springs, CO: Multnomah Books, 2010), 35.

[9]Beth Moore, *Jesus the One and Only* (Nashville, TN: Lifeway Press, 2000), 221.

[10]James Stewart, *The Strong Name* (Grand Rapids, MI: Baker Books, 1972), 55.

[11]*Charles H. Spurgeon's Autobiography,* vol. 1 (London: Passmore and Alabaster, 1897; reprinted edition, Pasadena, TX: Pilgrim Publications, 1992), 113.

[12]INSIGHTS by Bill Bright. June 11, 2003.

[13]Jared C. Wilson, *Gospel Wakefulness* (Wheaton, IL: Crossway, 2011), 204.

[14]"Rock of Ages," by Augustus Toplady. Public domain.

[15]F. W. Krummacher, *The Suffering Savior* (Chicago, IL: Moody Press, 1947), 399-400.

[16]Oswald Chambers, *My Utmost for His Highest* (New York: Dodd, Mead, & Company, 1935), 58.

[17]J. B. Phillips, *Your God Is Too Small* (Old LandMark Publishing, 2008).

[18]C. S. Lewis, *Prince Caspian: The Return to Narnia* (New York: Harper Collins, 1994), 141.

[19]From "O Worship the King," by Robert Grant. Public domain.

[20]John Piper, *Don't Waste Your Life* (Wheaton, IL: Crossway Books, 2013), 38.

[21]"Then Jesus Came," by Oswald J. Smith. Public domain.

[22]"Love Divine, All Loves Excelling," by Charles Wesley. Public domain.

[23]A. J. Gordon, *In Christ: The Believer's Union with His Lord* (Grand Rapids, MI: Baker Book House, 1964), 11-12.

[24]"Before the Throne of God Above," by Charitie L. Bancroft. Public domain.

[25]John R. W. Stott, quoted in David Bryant, *Christ Is All!* (New Providence, NJ: New Providence Publishers, 2004), 25.

CHAPTER THREE

[1] Brent Curtis and John Eldridge, *The Sacred Romance* (Nashville, TN: Thomas Nelson Publishers, 1997), 45.

[2] The "Iron Curtain" was a designation given to the political, ideological, and geographic barrier between Eastern Europe and Western Europe that was precipitated by the oversight of victorious Allied nations at the end of World War II. The Soviet Union cast a pall of repressive, atheistic ideology over almost all of Eastern Europe from 1945 until 1991, making evangelism difficult and dangerous.

[3] Timothy Keller, *The Reason for God* (New York: Riverhead Books, 2008), 200.

[4] William Tyndale, "A Pathway into the Holy Scripture," in *Doctrinal Treatises* (Cambridge: The University Press, 1848), 8. Style updated.

[5] Timothy Keller, Facebook post, March 12, 2014.

[6] Doug Banister, *The Word and Power Church* (Grand Rapids, MI: Zondervan, 1999), 143.

[7] The followers of Jesus were first called Christians in Antioch. See Acts 11:26.

[8] Paul E. Billheimer, *Destined for the Throne* (Minneapolis, MN: Bethany House / Christian Literature Crusade, 1975), 23.

[9] http://www.patheos.com/robertcrosby/2012/5/2/luther-called-this-verse-the-gospel-in-miniature.

[10] Unknown origin. Quoted in O. S. Hawkins, *The Joshua Code* (Nashville, TN: Thomas Nelson, 2012), 23.

[11] Larry D. Hart, *Truth Aflame* (Grand Rapids, MI: Zondervan, 2005), 102.

[12] F.B. Meyer from *The Secret of Guidance*, quoted in Charles R. Swindoll, *Meet Me in the Library* (Plano, TX: IFL Publishing, 2011), 45-46.

[13] F. W. Krummacher, *The Suffering Savior*, 52.

[14] See Rick Renner, *Sparkling Gems from the Greek* (Tulsa, OK: Teach All Nations, 2003), 63-64; 121-122.

[15] "The Solid Rock," by Edward Mote. Public domain.

[16] Charles H. Spurgeon, "The Exceeding Riches of Grace," in *Metropolitan Tabernacle Pulpit*, vol. 28 (1882, reprinted edition, Pasadena, TX: Pilgrim, 1973), 339.

[17] Harold Myra and Marshall Shelly, T*he Leadership Secrets of Billy Graham*, (Grand Rapids, MI: Zondervan Publishers, 2005), 193.

[18] John Piper, *Don't Waste Your Life* (Wheaton, IL: Crossway, 2003), 40.

[19] Italics in these verses have been added by the author.

[20] Raymond C. Ortlund, *The Gospel: How the Church Portrays the Beauty of Christ* (Wheaton, IL: Crossway Books, 2014), 15.

[21] "Upon the Gospel's Sacred Page," by John Bowering. Public domain. Bowering was a prominent British politician who served for a time as mayor of Hong Kong. He also wrote, "In the Cross of Christ I Glory."

[22] *John Wesley's Journal*, January 24, 1738. https://jamespedlar.wordpress.com/2011/05/21/four-john-wesley-quotes-everyone-should-know/.

[23] John Wesley, *The Journal of John Wesley* (Grand Rapids, MI: Christian Classics Ethereal Library, 2000). www.ccel.org/ccel/wesley/journal.vi.ii.xvi.

html?highlight+i,felt,my,heart,strangely,warmed#highlight.

[24] "Jesus, Thy Blood and Righteousness," by Nikolas von Zinzendorf, translated into English by John Wesley. Public domain.

[25] "How Does It Happen? Trajectories Toward an Adjusted Gospel," by R.Albert Mohler Jr. in Mark Dever, J. Ligon Duncan III, R. Albert Mohler Jr., C. J. Mahaney, *The Unadjusted Gospel* (Wheaton, IL: Crossway, 2014), 62.

[26] Larry D. Hart, *Truth Aflame*, 316.

[27] "Fairest Lord Jesus" translated by Joseph A. Seiss. Public domain.

[28] Raymond C. Ortlund, *Gospel: How the Church Portrays the Beauty of Christ*, 16.

[29] "Joy to the World, the Lord Is Come," by Isaac Watts. Public domain.

[30] Calvin Miller, *The Taste of Joy* (Downers Grove, IL: InterVarsity Press, 1983), 38.

CHAPTER FOUR

[1] Paul Washer, *The Gospel's Power and Message* (Grand Rapids, MI: Reformation Heritage Books, 2012) 63.

[2] Author unknown.

[3] The Gospel Coalition Confessional Statement, 2006.

[4] Matt Chandler with Jared Wilson, *The Explicit Gospel* (Wheaton, IL: Crossway, 2012), 82.

[5] Paul E. Billheimer, *Destined for the Throne*, (Fort Washington, PA: Christian Literature Crusade, 1975), 21-22.

[6] "There is a Redeemer," by Melody Green. © 1982, Universal Music Publishing Group.

[7] "There is Power in the Blood," by Lewis E. Jones. Public Domain.

[8] "The Amazingly Graced Life of John Newton" | www.christianitytoday.com/ch/2004/issue81/3.16html. Accessed July 22, 2015.

[9] John Pollock, *Amazing Grace: John Newton's Story* (San Francisco, CA: Harper & Row, 1981), 182.

[10] Matt Chandler with Jared Wilson, *The Explicit Gosel*, 142.

[11] Italics added. All quotations for this section are from the *Holman Christian Standard Bible*. Used by permission.

[12] "The Blood Will Never Lose Its Power," words and music by Andrae Crouch. © Copyright, 1966. Renewed 1994 by Manna Music, Inc. (ASCAP), 35255 Brooten Road, Pacific City, OR 97135. All rights reserved. Used by permission.

[13] "The Power of the Cross," words and music by Keith Getty and Stuart Townend. Copyright © 2005, Thankyou Music.

[14] Raymond C Ortlund, *The Gospel: How the Church Portrays the Beauty of Christ* (Wheaton, IL: Crossway Books, 2014), 18-19.

[15] Gary Tyra, *The Holy Spirit in Mission* (Downers Grove, IL: IVP Academic, 2011), 31.

[16] T. L. Osborn, *The Purpose of Pentecost* (Tulsa, OK: The Osborn Foundation, 1963), 105.

[17]Robert E. Coleman, *The Coming World Revival* (Wheaton, IL: Crossway Books, 1995), 155.

[18]John Wimber with Kevin Springer, *Power Evangelism* (San Francisco, CA: Harper and Row, 1986), 16.

[19]While the authenticity of the last several verses of the Gospel of Mark is debated by scholars, it is assumed to be authoritative by most Bible believers worldwide.

[20]T. L. Osborn, *The Harvest Call* (Tulsa, OK: The Voice of Faith, 1953), 143.

[21]Jerry Bridges, *The Transforming Power of the Gospel* (Colorado Springs, CO: NavPress, 2012), 127.

[22]"When I Survey the Wondrous Cross," by Isaac Watts. Public domain.

CHAPTER FIVE

[1]Robert A. Baker, *A Summary of Christian History* (Nashville, TN: Broadman Press, 1959), 309.

[2]Dietrich Bonhoeffer, *The Cost of Discipleship* (New York: Macmillan, 1967), 55.

[3]Jim Elliot, in Elisabeth Elliot, ed., *The Journals of Jim Elliot* (Old Tappan, NJ: Revell, 1978), 253.

[4]*The Baptist Faith and Message 2000*. www.sbc.net/bfm2000/bfm2000.asp.

[5]*The Statement of Fundamental Truths of the Assemblies of God*. http://www.org/top/beliefs/statement_of_fundamental_truths/sft_full.cfm.

[6]Wayne Grudem, *Systematic Theology* (Grand Rapids, MI: Zondervan, 1994), 718.

[7]Elisabeth Elliot, *Discipline: The Glad Surrender* (Grand Rapids, MI: Revell, 1982), 25

[8]Oswald Chambers, *My Utmost for His Highest* (Ulrichsville, OH: Barbour Publishing, n.d.), 141.

[9]William J. Arndt and F. Wilbur Gingrich, *A Greek-English Lexicon of the New Testament and Other Early Christian Literature* (Chicago, IL: The University of Chicago Press, 1957, 1969), 465.

[10]Larry D. Hart, 307.

[11]"The Royal Savior," Sermon #3229, Charles Spurgeon. Delivered February 1, 1872. Published December 22, 1910. *The Metropolitan Tabernacle Pulpit*. Volume 56, 3. www.spurgeongems.org.

[12]Robert E. Speer, *The Finality of Jesus Christ* (Grand Rapids, MI: Zondervan Publishing House, 1933, 1968), 257.

[13]Bill Bright, *The Joy of Sharing Jesus* (Colorado Springs, CO: Victor, 2005), 37.

[14]"Rescue the Perishing," by Fanny J. Crosby. Public domain.

[15]Billy Graham, *A Biblical Standard for Evangelists* (Minneapolis, MN: Worldwide Publications, 1983), 73.

[16]Timothy Keller, *Generous Justice* (New York: Penguin Group, 2010), 99.

[17]Matt Chandler and Michael Stetzer, *Recovering Redemption* (Nashville, TN: B&H Publishing Group, 2014), 52-53.

[18]Determinism is the teaching that all events are ultimately determined

by causes outside the human will. This concept shows up prominently in eastern religions and in the fatalistic philosophy of B. F. Skinner and others.

[19]Chuck Swindoll, Facebook entry, July 1, 2015.

[20]Jerry Bridges, *The Transforming Power of the Gospel* (Colorado Springs, CO, NavPress, 2012), 127.

[21]Thomas Chalmers, D.D., *The Expulsive Power of a New Affection* (Minneapolis, MN: Curiosmith, 1855, 2012).

[22]Dr. and Mrs. Howard Taylor, *Hudson Taylor's Spiritual Secret* (Chicago, IL: Moody Publishers, New Edition, 2009), 16.

[23]I've written extensively on the Judgment Seat of Christ, proposing that our final accountability to Jesus is one of the very strongest motivations for godly living. See David Shibley, *Living as if Heaven Matters* (Lake Mary, FL: Charisma House, 2007).

[24]Harry Reeder, "The Gospel-Driven Life," September 2, 2010, Providence Presbytery of the Presbyterian Church in America. http://www.providencepresbytery.org/articles.php?aid=55.

[25]"Jesus Paid It All," by Elvina M. Hall. Public domain.

CHAPTER SIX

[1]Sermon by Dale Evrist, June 7, 2015.

[2]Albert Mohler, Jr., "Trajectories toward an Adjusted Gospel," in Mark Dever, J. Ligon Duncan III, R. Albert Mohler Jr., C. J. Mahaney, *The Adjusted Gospel* (Wheaton, IL: Crossway, 2014), 50.

[3]Scott Hinkle, *Recapturing the Primary Purpose* (Frisco, TX: Scott Hinkle Outreach Ministries, 2005), 45.

[4]*Antinomianism* literally means "against law." It is an ancient heresy asserting that grace cancels any need for moral law. Paul was slanderously accused of propagating this teaching because of his strong emphasis on God's grace and the finished work of Christ as the sole means of salvation. Concerning those who accused him of promoting antinomianism Paul said, "Their condemnation is deserved" (Ro. 3:8, NIV).

[5]Al Mohler, "Moralism is Not the Gospel (But Many Christians Think It Is)", albertmohler.com. April 8, 2014. Accessed August 20, 2015.

[6]Quoted in Ravi Zacharias Facebook page, Nov. 12, 2014. Accessed August 20, 2015.

[7]Quoted in www.breakpointorg/bpcommentaries/entry/13/24570. Accessed August 20, 2015.

[8]See Chapter Eight, "Prosperity's Purpose," in David Shibley, *A Force in the Earth* (Lake Mary, FL: Creation House, 1989, 1997).

[9]A. W. Tozer, *The Pursuit of God* (CreateSpace Independent Publishing Platform, 2015), 22.

[10]John Calvin, *Institutes of the Christian Religion*, 2 vols., ed John T. McNeill, trans. Ford Lewis Battles (Philadelphia, PA: Westminster, 1960), 1:496 (II.xv.2).

[11]Jack W. Hayford, *Hayford's Bible Handbook* (Nashville, TN: Thomas Nelson

Publishers, 1995), 622.

[12]See Josh Packard and Ashleigh Hope, *Church Refugees* (Loveland, CO: Group Publishing, 2015).

[13]James Emery White, *Serious Times* (Downers Grove, IL: InterVarsity Press, 2004), 12.

[14]Rob Hoskins, *Hope Delivered* (Lake Mary, FL: Passio, 2012), 139, 150.

[15]John Piper, Third Lausanne Congress on World Evangelization, October 2010, http://tinyurl.com/7qocmvs (accessed August 17, 2015).

[16]Greg Gilbert, *What Is the Gospel?* (Wheaton, IL: Crossway, 2010), 109.

[17]See Nabeel Qureshi with Lee Strobel, *Seeking Allah, Finding Jesus* (Grand Rapids, MI: Zondervan, 2014).

[18]www.usw.salvationarmy.org/uws/www_torrance2.nsf/vw-sublinks/FCD98CD68ABFB1868825771D00178DE1. Accessed August 23, 2015.

[19]Over the years I've written three feature length articles addressing the challenge of universalism. These articles have appeared in *Charisma* and *Ministry Today* magazines. They may be accessed at www.charismamedia.com. Several concepts in this chapter appeared first in these articles and are reprinted by permission.

[20]Francis Chan, *Erasing Hell* (Colorado Springs, CO: David C. Cook, 2011), 145.

[21]www.biblebb.com/files/edwards/je-justice.htm. Accessed August 24, 2015

[22]Calvin Miller, *A View from the Fields* (Nashville, TN: Broadman Press, 1978), 94.

[23]John Piper, *Let the Nations Be Glad!* (Grand Rapids, MI: Baker Book House, 1993), 120.

[24]http://ministrytodaymag.com/ministry-today-archives/66-unorganized/7519-doctrine-of-demons. Accessed August 24, 2015.

[25]David Platt, *Radical* (Colorado Springs, CO: Multnomah Books, 2010), 159.

[26]Larry Stockstill, *Twenty-five Lines Around* (Baton Rouge, LA: Heartbeat Publishing, 1992), 2.

[27]G. K. Chesterton, "Illustrated London News," April 19, 1930.

[28]Nancy Pearcey, *Total Truth* (Wheaton, IL: Crossway, 2004, 2005), 18.

[29]G. K. Chesterton, *The Everlasting Man* (Garden City, NY: Image Books, 1955), 260-261.

[30]Os Guinness, *Renaissance: The Power of the Gospel However Dark the Times* (Downers Grove, IL: InterVarsity Press, 2014), 14.

CHAPTER SEVEN

[1]John Eldredge, *Wild at Heart* (Nashville, TN: Thomas Nelson, 2001), 32.

[2]"Send the Light," by Charles H. Gabriel. Public domain.

[3]"Divine Appointment at Subway," Global Advance email, August 26, 2015.

[4]Timothy Keller, *Center Church* (Grand Rapids, MI: Zondervan, 2012), 36.

[5]See John Stott, *For the Lord We Love: Your study guide to The Lausanne Covenant* (The Lausanne Movement, 2009).

[6]Michael Green, *Evangelism in the Early Church*. Quoted by Ed Stetzer. http://

www.christianitytoday.com/edstetzer/2014/July/morning-roundup-72214. html. Accessed August 25, 2015.

[7]"The Amsterdam Declaration," http://www.christianitytoday.com/ct/2000/augustweb-only/13.0.html. Accessed August 27, 2015.

[8]From *A Select Collection of Letters of the Late George Whitefield* (London: Edwards and Charles Dilly, 1772), 2:440. http://pastorhistorian. com.2014/07/09/evangelistic-letters-to-benjamin-franklin-from-george-whitefield/. Accessed August 27, 2015.

[9]Stephen Neill, *History of Christian Missions* (Middlesex, England: Penguin, 1964), 42-43.

[10]http://www. omf/?s=something+in+the+Gospel+worth+risking+Hudson+Taylor+&lang+en. Accessed August 27, 2015.

[11]http://www.christianitytoday.com/ct/2014/september/wrong-kind-of-christian-vanderbilt-university.html?start:3. Accessed August 27, 2015.

[12]Albert Mohler, *Culture Shift* (Colorado Springs, CO: Multnomah Books, 2008), 30.

[13]"The Amsterdam Declaration," Ibid., Accessed August 29, 2015.

[14]"The Millennial Manifesto," http://www.ad2000.org/celebrate/manifesto. htm.

[15]Vishal and Ruth Mangalwadi, *The Legacy of William Carey* (Wheaton, IL: Crossway Books, 1999), 85.

[16]http://thomranier.com/2015/02/fifteen-reasons-churches-less-evangelistic-today/. Accessed August 31, 2015.

[17]Deitrich Bonhoeffer, *The Cost of Discipleship* (New York: Touchstone, SCM Ltd., 1995, 1959), 211.

[18]Betty Lee Skinner, *Daws: The Story of Dawson Trotman* (Grand Rapids, MI: Zondervan Publishing House, 1975), 35.

[19]Edward K. Rowell, *1001 Quotes, Illustrations, and Humorous Stories for Preachers, Teachers, and Writers* (Grand Rapids, MI: Baker Books, 2008), 58.

[20]Nancy Pearcey, *Total Truth* (Wheaton, IL: Crossway Books, 2004, 2005), 125.

[21]"The Imperative of Apologetics: Evidence-Based Evangelism and Transforming Culture," Jim Burkett.

[22]John R. W. Stott, *Your Mind Matters* (Downers Grove, IL: InterVarsity Press, 1972), 13.

[23]Quoted by Michael Catt in Scott Dawson, editor, *The Complete Evangelism Guidebook* (Grand Rapids, MI: Baker Books, 2004), 54.

[24]Dick Eastman, *Love on Its Knees* (Old Tappan, NJ: Chosen Books, 1989), 19.

[25]This story is recounted in Joseph M. Stowell, *Following Christ* (Grand Rapids, MI: Zondervan, 1996), 130-131.

[26]Curtis Vaughan, *Ephesians: A Study Guide Commentary* (Grand Rapids, MI: Zondervan Publishing House, 1977), 128-129.

[27]Timothy Keller, *Center Church*, 44.

[28]Henry Drummond, *A Book of Daily Readings*, Selected and arranged by G. F. Maine (London: Collins, n.d.), 130.

[29]If you prayed to receive Christ as your Lord and Savior, I will be happy to send you a free copy of my book for new believers, *Now That You Are His.* Contact us at salvationprayer@globaladvance.org.

[30]H. Richard Niebuhr, quoted in D. Ivan Dykstra, *Who Am I? and Other Sermons* (Holland, MI: Hope College, 1983), 104.

[31]Robert Morris, Gateway Conference, October 20, 2014.

[32]*George Whitefield's Journals* (London: Banner of Truth Trust/Billings and Sons, Ltd., 1960), 352.

AFTERWORD

[1]"Am I a Soldier of the Cross?" by Isaac Watts. Public domain.

[2]http://www.ligonier.org/learn/seeing-gospel-word-god/. Accessed August 14, 2015.

[3]"Rescue the Perishing" by Fanny Crosby. Public domain.

[4]Quoted in John Piper, "The Supremacy of God in Missions through Worship," *Into All the World*, 2001 edition, 8.

ABOUT THE AUTHOR

David Shibley is founder and world representative for Global Advance. For over quarter century Global Advance has brought on-site training, resources, and encouragement to over 700,000 leaders in 97 nations, challenging these leaders to help fulfill the Great Commission. The author of more than 20 books,  David is a graduate of John Brown University and Southwestern Baptist Theological Seminary. He also holds an honorary doctorate from Oral Roberts University. He and his wife, Naomi, have been married since 1972. They have two married sons and five grandchildren.

GLOBAL ADVANCE

Equipping Leaders to Fulfill the Great Commission

For over a quarter century Global Advance has gone to many of the world's most difficult places:

- *convening* hundreds of thousands of leaders, equipping them, and putting a vision in their hearts and tools in their hands
- *connecting* isolated leaders in new networks to advance the cause of Christ
- *commissioning* leaders to reach and disciple their nations for Christ

Founded in 1990 by David Shibley, Global Advance is recognized today as a premier ministry providing training and resources for Christ's servants on the frontlines of the gospel's global advance.

As challenges to the church's mission intensify the future for the ministry of Global Advance has never been brighter.

You can make a world of difference for Jesus Christ. Partner with Global Advance. Lives will be changed. Leaders will be lifted. Nations will be impacted. Jesus will be honored.

GLOBAL ADVANCE
P.O. Box 742077
Dallas, Texas 75374-2077
972-771-9042

globaladvance.org

Global Advance: facebook.com/GlobalAdvance
David Shibley: facebook.com/davidshibleyblog/

Made in the USA
Lexington, KY
17 February 2016